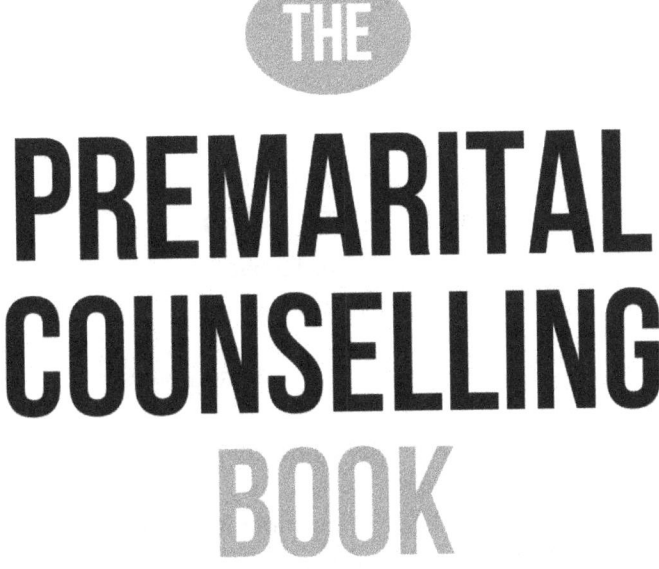

THE PREMARITAL COUNSELLING BOOK

A MARRIAGE PREPARATION MANUAL
TO HELP YOU SAY 'I DO' WITH CONFIDENCE

DESIGNED FOR PEOPLE WHO WANT TO BUILD
THEIR MARRIAGE ON CHRISTIAN VALUES

THE PREMARITAL COUNSELLING BOOK

By Tony Peters

Published by
T.P.PUBLICATIONS
4 Pegamoid Road.
London. N18 2NG

Copyright © 2024 by Tony Peters

ISBN: 978-1-874332-78-7 (Print)

Unless otherwise noted, Scripture quotations are taken from the
New King James Version. Copyright © 1979,1982.
Thomas Nelson, Inc.

Scriptures marked (NLT) are taken from the
New Living Translation. Copyright © 1996, 2004.
Tyndale House Publisher.

Scriptures marked (NIV) are taken from the
New International Version. Copyright © 1984, 2011.
Biblica, Inc.

Scriptures marked (ESV) are taken from the
English Standard Version. Copyright © 2008.
Crossway Bibles, Good News Publishers.

All rights reserved. No part of this book may be reproduced or transmitted in any form or by any means, electronic or mechanical, including photocopying, recording, or by any information storage and retrieval system—with the exception of brief excerpts in articles and reviews—without permission in writing from the Author or Publisher.

ENDORSEMENTS

WoW! What an incredible and inspiring 210 pages of a classic Marriage Preparation Manual shared in these critical times in a post-Christian world.

This much-needed seminal book by Dr. Tony Peters is a perfect resource for young couples seeking God's spiritual and moral compass in the area of Marriage Preparation. It is a clear road-map in a world that has lost its way both spiritually and morally.

The writer's classic definitions of God's knowledge, understanding and wisdom concerning marriage is brilliantly weaved into the full tapestry of this must-read book from start to finish. I personally found those definitions most refreshing throughout my gripping and compelling read.

Throughout this book I found Dr. Tony's simple but gripping writing style quite easy to read; and I fully agree with him when he so aptly asserts that his book "is an essential stepping stone to the extraordinary adventure that marriage is designed to be".

Finally, you will find Dr. Tony's compendium of biblical truth on the institution of marriage extremely riveting to the very end. It is a must-read book for all needing to find a "more excellent way"!

Apostle Richard & Elizabeth Mitchell
Global Missions International.
Cambridgeshire, UK.

At a time when there are so many misconceptions and mixups regarding God's original plan and purpose for the institution of marriage, this Premarital Counselling Manual by Pastor Tony Peters—a dear friend of mine for over thirty five years—will definitely help prospective couples who desire to have a fruitful and fulfilling marriage.

Bishop Paul Fadeyi
Grace Outreach Church.
England, U.K.

This Premarital Marriage Manual ought to be made compulsory for all pastors and parents to start training their children and wards in the union of marriage. It is unbelievable that we think 4 weeks of counselling or teaching before the wedding is enough.

We know that faith comes by hearing again and again. That's why parents must have a manual like this to help their children—and not thrust that responsibility to the Church alone.

This Premarital Marriage book is an excellent manual that I recommend to every pastor and parent, to use to train their children in the way to go, so that when they grow into adulthood they will not depart from it.

Bishop Segun Johnson
Liberty Ministries International.
London.

This is an excellent and comprehensive counselling Manual. I recommend it to all. I have been in Marriage Counseling for almost 40 years and found the contents to be biblical and very practical. Praise God and thank you, Pastor Tony Peters for this master piece. May Jehovah shine His light on all who read and apply the contents therein. Amen.

Rev. Solomon Adebara
President
Fountain Of Grace Ministries.
Ibadan, Nigeria.

TABLE OF CONTENT

INTRODUCTION	6
HOW TO USE THIS MANUAL	7

CHAPTER 1
WHAT PREMARITAL COUNSELLING WILL DO FOR YOU — 12

CHAPTER 2
THE BENEFITS OF A HEALTHY MARRIAGE — 17

CHAPTER 3
WHY DO YOU WANT TO GET MARRIED? — 21

CHAPTER 4
ARE YOU READY TO GET MARRIED? — 29

CHAPTER 5
COUPLE'S QUESTIONNAIRE — 33

CHAPTER 6
THE MARRIAGE MINDSET — 43

CHAPTER 7
HOW TO BUILD A SUCCESSFUL MARRIAGE — 55
- PRINCIPLE #1 — 55
- PRINCIPLE #2 — 63
- PRINCIPLE #3 — 69
- PRINCIPLE #4 — 89
- PRINCIPLE #5 — 97
- PRINCIPLE #6 — 104
- PRINCIPLE #7 — 131
- PRINCIPLE #8 — 137
- PRINCIPLE #9 — 141
- PRINCIPLE #10 — 155
- PRINCIPLE #11 — 163

CHAPTER 8
HOW TO ELIMINATE STRESS FROM YOUR WEDDING DAY — 172

CHAPTER 9
GOD'S WILL FOR YOUR MARRIAGE — 180
A BEAUTIFUL ADVENTURE — 193
Extra Scriptures to Ponder on — 195
Other Books by the Author — 198

INTRODUCTION

Let me begin by extending my heartfelt congratulations to you because you've decided to prepare yourself for one of the most important journeys of your life. Many couples never stop to consider how important premarital counselling is. But it is an essential stepping stone to the extraordinary adventure that marriage is designed to be.

Marriage is a lifelong commitment to meeting your partner's needs. It is embarking on a journey of continual nurture and support for each other until your assignment here ends. Marriage isn't a sprint; it is a marathon. The path to making your marriage a source of pride and joy is a journey that unfolds over time, not overnight.

By dedicating your time and honesty to this manual alongside your partner (if possible), you're making one of the wisest preparations for the dream marriage you both desire. Yes, achieving your dream marriage is possible, provided your dreams are grounded in reality, humility, discipline, and determination. No, your marriage won't be perfect, as perfection is an elusive human goal. However, it can be incredibly rewarding and fulfilling, brimming with joy and cherished memories. It can make you feel like the 'luckiest' and most blessed person alive on the planet.

Believe me; I wake up feeling this way every day. This sense of fulfilment isn't exclusive to me or to a few fortunate people; it's within reach for anyone willing to invest the time and necessary effort. Remember, greatness and value rarely come without dedication and hard work. Similar to cultivating a beautiful garden or becoming a skilled golfer, marriage demands time, effort, and continuous learning. It is a lifelong journey of tenacity, growth, and transformation. The good news is that you're taking the vital first steps by reading this book. Be rest assured that you won't regret it.

Rev. (Dr.) Tony Peters.

HOW TO USE THIS MANUAL

I want to assure you that you are doing the right thing. You got this manual because you value knowledge, understanding and wisdom. According to Solomon, anyone who values these three concepts is wise. The three words mean three distinctly different things.

- **Knowledge** is the **accumulation** of truths or facts.
- **Understanding** is the **assimilation** of truths or facts.
- **Wisdom** is the **application** of truths or facts.

You need all three to successfully navigate the maze that we call marriage. The **aim** of this manual is not just to present you with more great information, or to only help you understand the intricacies of the marriage journey, but to get you to **apply** and **practice** what you learn.

Implementation is Key

A lot of people know a lot of great things, but knowledge without implementation is like owning a top-of-the-range supercar and never learning to drive it. That's a waste of your resources. So, the goal is wisdom. Wisdom to implement and apply what you learn in this manual.

> **When wisdom enters your heart, and knowledge is pleasant to your soul, discretion will preserve you; and understanding will keep you...** (Proverbs 2:10-11.)

But for that to happen, you need to be very intentional. You can't afford to approach this material like a novel or a history book. This is a study Manual. The spaces in it are there for you to write down your **thoughts**, **ideas**, **decisions** and **prayers**. Trust me, you will come back to it again and again, and it will be very refreshing.

Using this Material

If you are still single, you can use it alone. It will get you thinking about your future; and it will help to clarify some areas of your life that require adjustments, change or growth. If, on the other hand, you are already contemplating marriage with a special person, you would benefit more if you go through it together. So make it a priority in your relationship.

Instead of sitting down every time you meet to watch Netflix, Disney movies or AppleTV, invest some time to get into alignment in this important area of your lives. Since your partner would invariably need to write down his or her thoughts and decisions too, it may pay you to invest in another copy of this manual.

Another great way—perhaps even the best way—to use this manual, is to go through it with a minister, counsellor, coach, or mature Christian; who can help you navigate difficult or unfamiliar concepts, and who can help you (and your partner) with accountability and focus.

If you need to take a driving test, you would spend hundreds of dollars and scores of hours taking driving lessons and reading through the Highway Code. Well, your future marriage is more important than a driving licence. So take this exercise even more seriously.

Don't forget to Pray

Give it all the thinking and praying time it needs. Don't rush through it just to fulfil all righteousness. Instead, be prayerful, be thoughtful, be thorough, be intentional, and be honest with yourself and your partner —if what you are reading requires further discussion.

If you give yourself wholeheartedly to the process, I promise that God would use this material to prepare you for the difficult but rewarding labour of building a successful lifelong marriage. How can I be so confident that it would work for you?

Firstly, because God's Word works every time you work it. Heaven and earth will pass away, but God's Word remains forever sure.

> Isaiah 40:8, says: **"The grass withers, the flower fades, but the word of our God stands forever."**

Secondly, I'm confident it would work for you, because I've seen it work in all types of marriages (including mine) for over 38 years.

So if you are ready to dive in and be intentional, say this prayer from your heart:

> *Dear Lord, I thank you for leading me to get this Marriage Preparation Manual. You said: Wisdom is the principle thing. So today, I ask that I would take a hold of your wisdom for marriage. As I study this material,*

open my eyes to your truth, and grant me the grace to do whatever you require of me. I now step forward by faith to take a hold of the destiny you have in store for me. I am grateful for my lifelong, joy-filled, and God-honouring Marriage. Thank you for the amazing journey you are preparing me to take. In Jesus' Name. Amen!

WHAT WE WILL COVER

In this course, we will cover several important aspects of building a strong lifelong marriage.

In Part 1, we will discuss:

- Why Premarital Counselling is Essential.
- What Premarital Counselling would do for you Personally.
- Your Reasons for wanting to get Married.
- Signs that you are Ready for Marriage.
- Important Questions for Couples to discuss.

In Part 2 of the manual, we will discuss what it means to approach marriage with maturity and the right mindset. We will discuss:

- Understanding Marriage from God's perspective.
- Working on yourself and your Marriage.
- Making sure that your expectations are realistic.
- Making sure you've heard from God and have His peace.
- Understanding that you both carry baggage and must learn how to minimise its effect on your relationship.
- Embracing the reality of the Marriage Covenant, and
- Recognising the five stages or seasons of Marriage.

Next, we will explore the **eleven** major areas that can hinder or help you to build a strong Marriage. We will learn what they are, and how we can navigate them successfully. Here, I will give you my best advice on:

1.) Developing Clear Marital Vision.

2.) Understanding and Embracing your Differences.

3.) Conflict Resolution.

4.) Healthy Ways to Communicate.

5.) How to Make Good Decisions.

6.) How to Share Roles and Responsibilities.

7.) How to Manage Your Finances.

8.) Functioning as a Team.

9.) How to Enjoy Sexual Intimacy.

10.) Dealing Wisely with Family and In-laws.

11.) Keeping God at the centre of your Home and Marriage.

Finally, I will touch on how you can eliminate stress on your wedding day; and how you can prepare yourself for a life of joy, fulfilment, and a lifelong adventure.

CHAPTER 1

WHAT PREMARITAL COUNSELLING WILL DO FOR YOU

> *"Plans fail for lack of counsel, but with many advisers, they succeed."* (Proverbs 15:22.) NIV.

After counselling couples for over 35 years, I am sad to say that our society demands more from teenagers who just want to drive a car than we do from couples who want to get married. We seem to forget that couples who get married today will be the ones raising the next generation of leaders and nation-builders tomorrow.

If a young person in our society wants to learn to cut hair for a living, he or she would have to go for months of tuition and practice to qualify. On the other hand, if that same person wants to get married, build a home, and parent the next generation of children; all they have to do is walk into a marriage registry, pay a few pounds and walk out with a certificate that says they qualify to take on one of life's most difficult task. That can't be right!

For what it is worth, I believe that our cavalier attitude towards the marriage institution is partly to blame for its high rate of failure in our society today. Starting a relationship that is intended to end in marriage is a very complicated thing. No one can tell you everything you need to know or do to make a success of it, because everyone's situation and circumstances are different.

Nevertheless, there are several important reasons why you should consider investing a lot of time and effort into preparing yourself extensively for marriage. Even if you are already in the heat of a loving relationship, there are plenty of good reasons to go back to the foundation and underpin it on the rock of God's immutable wisdom.

Here are some great reasons why premarital counselling is essential.

1. It Builds Strong Foundations Between You.

Just as a solid foundation is crucial for a sturdy building, a strong foundation is essential for a successful marriage. Premarital counselling allows you to delve into your values, beliefs, and goals as a couple, and identify areas where you may need to compromise or find balance. By establishing a strong foundation based on shared values, trust, and mutual understanding, you'll be better equipped to weather challenges that may arise in the future.

2. It Unveils Your Deepest Expectations.

Each person enters a marriage with their own set of expectations and beliefs. Premarital counselling helps you and your partner uncover and discuss these expectations openly. You will explore topics such as finances, career aspirations, family planning, roles and responsibilities, and more. By aligning your expectations and discussing potential conflicts or differences in advance, you can proactively address these issues and find common ground.

3. It Enhances Your Communication.

Effective communication is vital for any relationship. Counselling provides a safe space for you and your partner to learn and practice healthy communication skills. It's an opportunity to explore your communication styles, learn how to express your needs and understand how to resolve conflicts constructively. If you strengthen your communication skills at this point of your relationship, dealing with challenges in the future will be less stressful.

4. It Helps You Develop Good Relational Skills.

Successful marriages require specific skills and tools. Premarital counselling equips you with these essential relationship skills. You'll learn problem-solving techniques, effective conflict resolution, active listening, and more. By acquiring and practising these skills early on, you can navigate challenges and maintain a healthy, thriving relationship.

5. It Helps You Resolve Historic Unresolved Issues.

Many people carry unresolved issues or emotional baggage from previous relationships into their marriage. Premarital counselling provides an opportunity to address and heal these issues before they impact your relationship negatively. A skilled counsellor can guide you through the process of healing, forgiving, and letting go; allowing you to enter your marriage with emotional clarity and readiness.

6. It Helps You Address Your Financial Compatibility.

Finances can be a common source of conflict in marriages. Premarital Counselling allows you and your partner to openly discuss your financial values, attitudes, and goals. You get to explore topics like budgeting, saving, debt, and good financial planning. By understanding each other's perspectives and finding ways to work together a solid money foundation for your marriage can be achieved.

7. It Strengthens Your Commitment To Each Other.

Marriage is a lifelong commitment, and Premarital Counselling can help solidify your commitment to each other. It encourages you to reflect on your readiness for marriage, your dedication to the relationship, and your willingness to invest the necessary effort to make the marriage successful.

8. It Helps You Nurture Emotional Intimacy.

Premarital Counselling provides a safe environment for you and your partner to deepen your emotional connection. Through guided exercises and discussions, you'll learn how to express love, support, and vulnerability. If you take the time to build emotional intimacy now, you'll be setting the stage for an emotionally rich and fulfilling partnership.

9. It Helps You Explore Your Sexual Expectations.

Premarital Counselling allows you to discuss your expectations, desires, and concerns regarding physical intimacy. When you frankly address your expectations, you can prepare the ground for healthy sexual practices in the future. Discussing these and other issues candidly, can reduce anxiety and create stronger bonds of trust.

10. It Prepares You For Life Transitions.

Marriage often involves various life transitions, such as moving in together, starting a family, or blending families. Premarital Counselling can help you navigate these transitions more smoothly. You can explore topics like adjusting to living together, establishing shared routines and responsibilities, and preparing for parenthood.

11. It Can Offer Support From a Neutral Third Party.

Premarital Counselling also offers the invaluable support and guidance of a trained professional or Minister. The counsellor acts as a neutral third party who can provide objective insights, facilitate discussions, and offer guidance tailored to your specific needs. Having a knowledgeable or experienced professional guiding you through tough discussions can be extremely beneficial and revealing.

A Word of Caution

It's important to remember that Premarital Counselling is not a guarantee against challenges or conflicts in your marriage. However, it significantly enhances your preparedness and equips you with the necessary tools to tackle them more effectively. By investing in Premarital Counselling, you are prioritising the success, happiness and longevity of your future marriage.

If you embrace this opportunity, it will not only benefit your current relationship but also set a positive precedent for growth and open communication throughout your life's journey. In short, Premarital Counselling is an investment worth making to build a strong and fulfilling marriage partnership, that will stand the test of time.

Your Premarital Journal

What thoughts, ideas, decisions and prayer points would you like to keep a record of, after reading this chapter? Write them in the space below and discuss it with your spouse.

CHAPTER 2

THE BENEFITS OF A HEALTHY MARRIAGE

"Then the LORD God said, "It is not good for the man to be alone. I will make a helper who is just right for him."
(Genesis 2:18.) NLT.

A healthy marriage can bring numerous benefits to couples who invest the time and energy to build one. As you read through some of the key benefits of a healthy marriage, let them paint a picture of what is desirable and possible for you.

1. **Emotional support:** A healthy marriage provides a deep emotional bond and support system. Your spouse becomes a confidant, offering comfort, understanding, and encouragement during challenging times. This emotional support can significantly contribute to your overall well-being.

2. **Improved physical health:** A strong marriage can positively impact your physical well-being. Research suggests that happily married individuals tend to have lower rates of cardiovascular diseases, better immune function, and a longer life expectancy compared to those who are unmarried or in unhealthy marriages.

3. **Financial stability:** Marriage often brings financial benefits, such as shared expenses, dual incomes, and tax advantages. Couples can work together to set financial goals, manage finances effectively, and build wealth. This often provides a greater sense of security and financial stability.

4. **Enhanced personal growth:** A healthy marriage can serve as a strong catalyst for personal growth and self-improvement. In a supportive partnership, couples encourage and motivate each other to pursue their individual goals, explore new interests, and develop new skills—which in turn leads to personal fulfilment and growth.

5. **Better conflict resolution skills:** In a healthy marriage, couples learn to navigate conflicts and disagreements effectively. Developing

strong communication and conflict resolution skills not only strengthens the marital bond between you but translates into improved relationships with others too.

6. **Mental health benefits:** A healthy marriage can have a positive effect on your mental health. The emotional bond and sense of belonging within a marriage can help alleviate stress, reduce anxiety and depression symptoms, and promote overall psychological well-being.

7. **Stronger social connections:** Being part of a healthy marriage expands your social network. You gain access to your spouse's family and friends, and you may engage in joint social activities. This broader support system can enhance your sense of belonging, social connectedness, and overall life satisfaction.

8. **Greater resilience:** When facing life's challenges, having a healthy marriage can provide a significant buffer for you. The emotional support, teamwork, and shared problem-solving skills developed in a marriage can help you weather storms, bounce back from setbacks, and overcome obstacles more effectively.

9. **Increased joy or happiness:** Studies consistently show that couples with healthy marriages tend to report higher levels of happiness and life satisfaction. The companionship, love, and shared experiences in a healthy marriage contribute to a greater sense of joy and fulfilment in life.

10. **Stability for children:** If you decide to have children, marriage provides a stable and nurturing environment for their upbringing. Children raised in stable marital relationships tend to have better academic performance, emotional well-being, and overall life satisfaction.

A healthy marriage requires continuous effort, commitment, and open communication from both partners. Each individual's experience of marriage is unique, and it's essential to approach marriage with realistic expectations and a willingness to grow together as a couple. Nevertheless, investing in your marriage can yield these powerful benefits and more, leading to a more fulfilling and rewarding life together.

COUPLES DISCUSSION POINTS

- Which of the benefits above do you think you will require help with in your relationship?

  _____

  _____

- Did you experience or see any of these benefits playing out in your parent's marriage or relationship growing up? If so, which ones?

  _____

- How important is it to you to enjoy the ten benefits above in your marriage and home life?

  _____

Your Premarital Journal

What thoughts, ideas, decisions and prayer points would you like to keep a record of after reading this chapter? Write them down in the space below:

CHAPTER 3

WHY DO YOU WANT TO GET MARRIED?

Two are better than one, because they have a good reward for their labour. (Ecclesiastes 4:9.)

Before you get married you should check that you are doing so for the right reasons. Why do you want to get married? Is it because you have a lot of love to give your spouse or because you are afraid of being left out? Are you getting married just to please the people who've been pressuring you, or to make a loving home with someone you really love and adore?

Check your heart, because anything done with the wrong motive or for the wrong reasons, is inevitably built on sinking sand. In my best-selling book for singles (Maximising Your Season of Singleness), I share ten reasons not to jump into marriage and 9 good reasons to seek to get married.

Here are some of the bad or silly reasons people get married. Don't walk the aisle until you can cross your heart and say, "I'm not getting married for any of these unhealthy reasons".

1. To Escape a Dysfunctional Home.

Many people see marriage as their only way out of a bad home situation. But even so, your focus (when deciding to get married) should never be what you are running away from, but what you are going into. Statistically, people who come from a dysfunctional background are more likely to repeat or enable the same kind of dysfunction in their own homes. Why? Here is my theory. They put more of their energy into escaping from home than they put into making sure that they are ready for a healthier relationship. Therefore, never get married to escape a dysfunctional home situation. Rather, get married because you are ready to build a far better home than the one you came from. Get married because you've learnt from the mistakes your parents made and have developed the maturity and capacity to do things differently—or better.

2. Because All Your Friends Are Getting Married.

Just as our fingers are not all equal, people are not all the same. We have different needs at different times. We mature at different ages. We walk different paths and we have different destinies. Therefore, it doesn't make sense to allow your friends to pressure you into doing anything that doesn't suit you, or that you are not ready for. Walk your own path under God's guidance and you are more likely to get what you and God want for your life. In other words, don't let your friends dictate your actions. After all, they are not going to be there to help you, if things turn sour.

3. To Rebel Against Your Parents.

In the United Kingdom, where I live, the number of teenagers who leave home every year to cohabit with 'friends' or start a long-term relationship is alarming. However, studies from around the world show that young people who rebel against their parents also tend to rebel against the marriage institution—since marriage is governed by strict rules and values too. So, rebelling against your parents is not a good reason for getting married. Dealing with your tendency to rebel and learning to live within certain boundaries will place you on a better platform for married life. Because whether you know it or not, marriage hardly ever works well for people who hate boundaries and self-discipline.

4. To Improve Your Self-esteem.

Unfortunately, some people hope that marriage will make them feel better about themselves, or give meaning to their life. What they don't realise is that marriage has a way of magnifying what's in you—good or bad. If you are already feeling negative about yourself or your life, you are likely to be a drag on your spouse because you are emotionally unstable. Trust me; that will only make you feel worse about yourself. So work on your issues before you walk down the aisle—so that you can be an asset and not a liability in your marriage. An asset here, is anyone who increases your joy, your sense of gratitude, or your net worth. That's what you want to be to your spouse.

5. Pressure From Your Partner.

If your partner is pressuring you to get married, it is often because you've been together for too long. In which case, you need to decide whether you should continue the relationship or not; because it is not fair to keep stringing your partner along if you are not ready for marriage. At other times the pressure is in the form of emotional blackmail. One partner begins to say things like, "If you don't marry me, I will kill myself" or, "What am I going to do without you in my life?" Don't yield, because you will never really be happy; and you will likely hate your partner for it in the future.

6. You're Afraid You're Getting Too Old.

Again remember that it is better to get married at forty-five and enjoy thirty years of blissful marriage than to rush into a bad one at twenty-five and be looking for a way out by thirty. No marriage stands a chance if it is based on fear. If you are a child of God, He will take care of you and make sure that His will for your life comes to pass at the right time—and not a day too late.

7. There is a Baby On The Way.

Whenever a baby is involved in a premarital relationship, my gut instinct is to encourage the couple to get married and give that child a loving stable home. But even then, the baby would not be my only reason. I want them to give the baby a loving stable home, not a dysfunctional abusive circus. So, the baby (as important as it is) is secondary; but the marriage relationship is primary. Why? Because I would rather have a child living with one parent and visiting the other, than have that child damaged for life by two careless or irresponsible parents.

8. Pressure From Parents And Friends.

Our parents almost always want the best for us. But there must come a time when they step back from their role as parents and take on an adviser's role. If you are over twenty-one and your parents are still putting pressure on you to do things their way, it's probably time to sit them down and ask them kindly and respectfully to back off. Don't allow your parents or your relatives to put pressure on you to marry before you are ready to give it your all. It's just not fair to your spouse.

9. To Have Plenty of Free Sex.

Many people get married because they think it will be their ticket to hourly sex. Well, that's just not reality. In the real world, married people go to work, have bad days, get tired, get angry, come home late, travel without their spouse, have babies that keep them awake all night, and do a thousand and one other things. So, if it's all about sex for you, you are sure to be disappointed. Get married to serve and care for your spouse and great sex will be included in the package.

10. To Inherit Your Partner's Wealth.

Some people (believe it or not) go into marriage hoping to inherit the wealth of their spouse. They may not really love the person, but are willing to pretend that they do while they wait to inherit all their wealth. This is not only grossly unfair to the spouse, but massively deceitful. It's wrong and it's sinful! And, it is an abomination to God. Believe me; people who do this never really get away with it. Instead, they open themselves up to painful universal justice!

Healthier And Better Reasons To Get Married

In the same way that people get married for unhealthy reasons, there are healthy reasons to get married too. Ask yourself whether these are some of your main reasons for wanting to get married. If they are, your motives are on the right track.

You want to get married because:

1. You Are Convinced it's God's Will To Get Married.

If you are a Christ-follower, you are called to find out what His will for your life is—and to do it. Anything you do outside of God's will is vanity and a waste. So you must be persuaded that the marriage you are embarking upon is God's perfect will for your life. If you are, you have a great reason to get married.

2. You've Found the person you can love for the rest of your life.

Marriage is a marathon, not a 100-metre sprint. In addition, divorce is not a pretty option for any child of God. So you must be committed for the long haul. You must believe that you have found your soulmate and that no challenge thrown at you can dampen the love that God has put in your heart for your partner. If this is what you believe, you have another great reason to walk down the aisle with your spouse.

3. You are ready to start—or take good care of—a family.

Many couples turn to marriage because they believe that they are in love. But love alone does not make for a good marriage. Needs have to be met; responsibilities need to be shared; and progress needs to be made. So, if you don't have a stable job to take care of the family needs (especially if you are a man); or if you are ill-equipped to take care of the home (especially if you are a woman), your marriage can turn out to be a bed of thorns instead of a garden of roses. But if these issues are sorted in your heart, you have a fine reason to marry.

4. You are ready to meet your partner's needs in a mature and sacrificial way.

We generally get married to meet a handful of our deepest felt needs: Needs for love, affection, sex, security, companionship, affirmation, and so on. The number one reason for marital conflict is often a feeling of disappointment that those deep-seated needs are not being met. The solution therefore should be obvious: Discover your partner's deepest needs and commit yourself to meeting them in your marriage. When you are ready to do that, you are top marriage material.

5. You are willing to make adjustments for the sake of your spouse.

Marriage works best when there is a willingness to change. Rigid and inflexible people don't make for good spouses. Two totally different people can only become one as they complement, adapt and adjust to each other. If you are ready to make some positive adjustments to accommodate your spouse's uniqueness, and if you are mature enough to make good compromises, you are ready to get married. If not, you are not ready for marriage. It's that simple!

6. You are prepared to stretch and mature as a person.

Marriage is like a top University; it will stretch and test you. Your relationship with your spouse would challenge your beliefs, try your patience, verify your commitment and test your love to the limit. But that's all part of the beauty of a great marriage. If you don't want to be tested, don't go to a 'top University'. If you are ready to be stretched, you are a candidate for marriage.

7. The Kingdom of God will benefit from your marriage.

I always feel sad when very committed members of the local church lose their passion for God and for His Kingdom because they got married. The Bible teaches us that 'two are better than one'. And, Solomon tells us why. He says, "...their labour would be more satisfying." Or, you could say that their combined effort should produce much more fruit, than their individual effort. In other words, if you see your marriage as a tool to do more for God and not less, you have the right mindset to get married.

8. You are spiritually, emotionally and physically whole and prepared.

Marriage is tough enough without having to cope with an insecure or dysfunctional spouse. Thus, a good time to tie the knot is when you've allowed God to straighten you out. It's when you've been through the fire and the grinder; when you've mellowed because you've been humbled under the mighty hand of God; and when you've surrendered everything to Him. If that sounds like your life history, you are a candidate for marriage.

9. You know that marrying this particular person is God's perfect will for you both.

Why? Because you have a specific word or promise from the Holy Spirit.

How to Evaluate Your Answers.

If you can confidently say 'yes' to **six** or **seven** of the **nine** reasons I have highlighted above, you are well on your way to becoming a great marriage material. If you can't do so at the moment, I want to encourage you to make each point a prayer project. Take the issue to God daily—for a few months—until you sense that the change has taken place in your mind and in your heart.

Go over these **healthy reasons** again and promise yourself to work on each one of them until they become a part of you. People who have good reasons for doing whatever they do, often stick with it, until it is done. They are also the ones who succeed in the end.

Your Premarital Journal

What thoughts, ideas, decisions and prayer points would you like to keep a record of after reading this chapter? Write them in the space below:

CHAPTER 4

ARE YOU READY TO GET MARRIED?

Here are some general indicators that suggest you may be ready to get married. If you are a person of faith, it is also important to ask God for His perfect timing—and that the person you wish to marry is His perfect will for your life.

Read the following indicators and give yourself a mark between 1 and 5. If you are already in a serious relationship, go through the same exercise with your partner.

1 = Very Poor.

2 = Poor.

3 = Okay.

4 = Nearly there.

5 = 100% there.

1. Emotional maturity:

You have developed a strong sense of emotional maturity and are able to handle the ups and downs of a long-term commitment.

2. Shared values:

You and your partner share similar values, goals, and aspirations, which provide a solid foundation for building a life together.

3. Effective communication:

You have developed healthy communication patterns, including the ability to express your needs, listen actively, and resolve conflicts constructively.

4. Mutual respect: ☐

You and your partner have a deep respect for each other's individuality, opinions, values and boundaries.

5. Trust and honesty: ☐

There is a high level of trust and honesty in your relationship, and you both feel secure in each other's fidelity and commitment.

6. Wholistic Compatibility: ☐

You have spent enough time together (say, 12 to 18 months) to ensure that you are compatible in terms of goals, values, interests, lifestyles, character and spiritual maturity.

7. Financial compatibility: ☐

You have discussed and aligned your financial goals, spending habits, and approaches to money management.

8. Supportive partnership: ☐

You and your partner consistently support each other's personal growth, dreams, and ambitions, fostering an environment of mutual support and encouragement.

9. Problem-solving skills: ☐

You have successfully navigated through challenging situations as a couple and have demonstrated the ability to find solutions together.

10. Family and social integration: ☐

You and your partner have integrated well into each other's families and social circles, and you feel comfortable and accepted by the important people in each other's lives.

11. Long-term commitment: ☐

You have had open and honest conversations about your expectations for the future and are both committed to a lifelong partnership.

12. Inner conviction: ☐

You have a deep inner conviction that you are ready to make this commitment and can envision a fulfilling future with your partner.

Evaluating The Result Of The Exercise Above

This list is not exhaustive and the decision to get married should ultimately be based on your judgment, feelings, and the unique dynamics of your relationship. However, it's important to engage in open and honest conversations with your partner about the 12 **issues** above, and your readiness for marriage. It helps to seek guidance from trusted loved ones or professional counsellors—if needed.

The minimum mark you can give yourself is 12. The maximum is 60.

12–25 Marks mean: You are in no way ready to get married. Go and work on every area mentioned above and give yourself time to mature in every way. If possible, get a mentor to help.

26–38 Marks mean: You still have a lot of work to do, but you are on your way. Go over the weak areas of your assessment and get support to change them. Make these areas a prayer project.

39–50 Marks mean: You are almost ready to take the plunge. But if you take it right now, you may struggle a bit. Give yourself a few months to improve your assessment scores before committing to a marital relationship. Don't rush!

51–60 Marks mean: You are probably ready to get married when you connect to the right person. Just make sure that your partner is as prepared as you are. So, encourage them to take the test too. A healthy marriage always takes two!

Your Premarital Journal

What thoughts, ideas, decisions and prayer points would you like to keep a record of after reading this part of the manual? Write them in the space below:

CHAPTER 5

COUPLE'S QUESTIONNAIRE

One valuable tool that can help you evaluate where you and your partner are when it comes to your relationship is the **Premarital Questionnaire**. I want to encourage you to go through this Premarital questionnaire carefully because it will help you in several ways:

1. **Enhancing your Communication:** The premarital questionnaire will encourage you to discuss important topics openly, improve your communication skills and set a positive tone for your future marital dialogues. It will encourage discussions about important topics that might not have come up otherwise.

2. **Evaluating your Compatibility:** The premarital questionnaire can help you evaluate your compatibility in areas, such as values, communication styles, and life goals. It can help you understand where you align well and where you may need to work on your relationship before you tie the knot.

3. **Resolving Areas of Conflict:** These questionnaires often address potential sources of conflict in advance. They allow you to practice your conflict resolution skills now and establish healthy patterns for future challenges you are likely to face.

4. **Financial Planning:** They address financial matters and promote financial transparency, helping you to understand each other's financial habits, expectations, and goals. This can prevent financial surprises and money conflicts down the road.

5. **Assess Emotional Readiness:** Premarital questionnaires can help you assess your emotional readiness for marriage, ensuring that you are mentally prepared for the responsibilities and challenges of married life.

6. **Set Expectations:** The Premarital questionnaire will allow you to discuss and set clear expectations regarding your roles, responsibilities, and commitments in the marriage. This, in turn, reduces misunderstandings when you get married.

7. **Strengthen the Marriage Bond:** The premarital questionnaire is a positive tool for you to invest in your long-term success and happiness. It provides a structured way to evaluate and strengthen your relationship. Going through the questionnaire together can foster a sense of teamwork and collaboration which can strengthen the emotional bond between the two of you for years to come.

Couples Questionnaire

Below is a detailed questionnaire with several relevant questions covering 25 major aspects of marital relationships. I encourage you to go through it with your partner.

1. **Personal Values and Beliefs:**

    - What are your core values and spiritual beliefs, and how do they align with your partner's?

    _____

    - How important is being a contributing part of a Christian Community to you, and how do you plan to incorporate it into your marriage?

    _____

2. **Communication:**

    - How do you handle conflicts and disagreements in your relationship?

    _____

    - Are you comfortable sharing your thoughts and feelings openly with your partner?

    _____

    - How do you feel about active listening and empathetic communication in your relationship?

3. **Financial Matters:**
   - What are your individual financial goals and habits?

   - Are there any financial debts or obligations that you haven't discussed with your partner?

   - Have you discussed your financial expectations, budgeting, and who would manage your money?

4. **Family and Children:**
   - What are your expectations regarding the number of children you'd like to have and their upbringing?

   - How do you plan to balance family time with personal and career goals?
   - What do you feel your roles as parents in the future would be?

5. **Career and Ambitions:**
   - What are your career aspirations, and how do they align with your partner's?

   - How do you plan to support each other's career goals and maintain a work-life balance?

6. **Intimacy and Affection:**
   - How do you express affection, love, and intimacy in your relationship?

   - What is your dominant 'love language'?

- What is your partner's dominant 'love language'?

- What are your expectations regarding physical intimacy, including frequency and boundaries (i.e. Sexual acts that you find distasteful)?

7. **Conflict Resolution:**

- How have you handled major conflicts in your relationship, and what have you learned from them?

- What strategies do you plan to use for resolving conflicts constructively in your marriage?

8. **Family Background and Influence:**

- How have your family backgrounds and upbringing influenced your values and expectations in relationships?

- Are there any family dynamics or issues that may affect your marriage?

9. **Leisure Activities:**

- What are your favourite leisure activities, and how do you plan to spend quality time together?

- How do you feel about pursuing individual interests while maintaining shared activities?

10. **Roles and Responsibilities:**

- What are your expectations regarding gender roles and responsibilities in your marriage?

- How do you plan to share household chores, financial responsibilities, and decision-making?

___

11. **Health and Well-being:**
    - How do you prioritise physical and mental health in your life?

    ___

    - How will you support each other's health and well-being in your marriage?

    ___

12. **Trust and Boundaries:**
    - What does trust mean to you, and how do you build and maintain it in a relationship?

    ___

    - Do you know each other's personal boundaries, and how will you respect them going forward?

    ___

    - What boundaries, if any, do you have regarding interactions with the opposite sex?

    ___

13. **Past Relationships:**
    - Have you had a detailed discussion of your past relationships, including what happened and what you learnt from them?

    ___

    - Are there any unresolved issues or emotional baggage from previous relationships that may affect your marriage? (e.g. children, joint property ownership or spiritual soul ties.)

    ___

14. **Time Management:**
    - How do you manage your time individually, and how will you prioritise time together as a couple?

- Are there any commitments or obligations that may affect your availability for each other?

15. Extended Family:

- How do you plan to manage relationships with extended family members?

- Are there any boundaries or expectations regarding your involvement with each other's families?

16. Parenthood and Parenting Styles:

- How do you envision your roles as parents, and what are your parenting styles?

- Have you discussed important parenting decisions, such as discipline, education, and values?

17. Personal Growth:

- How do you both plan to encourage self-improvement and personal growth in the future?

- Are there any personal development goals you'd like to pursue together? (e.g. Further education or learning new skills.)

18. Technology and Social Media:

- How do you plan to manage the use of technology, social media, sports, and television in your relationship?

- Do you have any boundaries or expectations regarding privacy and online interactions? (e.g. with people of the opposite sex.)

19. **Caregiving Responsibilities:**
    - How do you plan to support each other in times of illness or family caregiving responsibilities?

    - Have you discussed potential challenges related to health and caregiving—for yourselves or family members?

20. **Resilience and Coping Strategies:**
    - How do you both cope with stress, setbacks, or unexpected life challenges?

    - Are there support systems or strategies you rely on during difficult times? If not, what will you do about it from now?

    - Are your coping strategies conducive or destructive to your Marriage? Do you need help to improve your responses?

21. **Hobbies and Interests:**
    - What are your hobbies and interests, and how do they complement or differ from your partner's?

    - What can you put in place to continue to appreciate and support each other's passions?

22. **Emotional Support:**
    - How do you provide emotional support to each other during difficult times?

- Are there specific ways you prefer to receive emotional support from your partner?

23. Adventure and Exploration:

- Do you have a sense of adventure, and how do you plan to explore new experiences together?

- What is your attitude toward travel and exploring as a couple?

24. Relationship Expectations:

- What are your expectations regarding commitment, fidelity, and the longevity of your marriage?

- How do you plan to nurture and maintain your relationship when life gets hectic?

25. Reflection on Compatibility:

- Based on your answers to the previous questions, what strengths and areas of growth do you see in your relationship?

- What steps will you take to strengthen your compatibility and readiness for marriage?

This comprehensive premarital questionnaire can serve as a valuable tool for you to explore various aspects of your relationship, identify potential areas of concern, and foster open and constructive communication as you prepare for the marriage of your dreams.

COUPLES DISCUSSION POINTS

- If there were questions that require more discussion time with your spouse, write them here so you don't forget.

_____

_____

_____

- Set a date (when you have 60-90 minutes) to go over your answers together. Highlight any areas of potential disagreement or conflict. Keep going back to them until you get a breakthrough.

_____

_____

_____

Your Premarital Journal

What thoughts, ideas, decisions and prayer points would you like to keep a record of after reading this part of the manual? Write them in the space below:

CHAPTER 6

THE MARRIAGE MINDSET

Understanding Marriage from God's Perspective

"For this reason a man shall leave his father and mother and be joined to his wife, and the two shall become one flesh."

Ephesians 5:31.

The way God sees marriage is so different from the way our society sees it. When God instituted marriage, He designed it to last 'till death do us part'. There were no 'ifs' or 'buts' in His intentions. Furthermore, God instituted and ordained marriage as a sacred duty for anyone wishing to enter into it.

In Ephesians 5, Paul compares the relationship between a husband and wife to that of Christ and His Church. This divine relationship between Christ and His Church models the commitment and sacrificial love required in marriage. In other words, marriage is designed to be patterned after the sacrifice of Christ for His Church.

Therefore, as Christ died for the Church (which is His Bride), a husband is called to be willing to die for his bride too. Similarly, as the Church honours and submits to Christ, a wife is called to respect and submit to her husband. This mystery is a divine pattern that requires a revelation from God to comprehend and embrace. But if you understand it and work to align your heart and your will with it, you cannot fail to nurture a really beautiful and powerful marriage.

Here are 9 crucial things to ponder and embrace, about the nature of marriage:

1. MARRIAGE IS A SPIRITUAL UNION

The Bible helps us to understand that: *"That which is born of the flesh is flesh, and that which is born of the Spirit is spirit."* (John 3:6.) Another way of saying this, is that a man's creation comes from his natural essence. So it's called flesh or carnal in the Bible. Similarly, God's creations come from His spirit essence. So it's called Spirit.

Since marriage was first initiated, instituted and ordained by God, it is a spiritual and sacred union. Why? Because it came from the spiritual essence of God, who is a Spirit being. That means marriage is not a personal, cultural or societal construct; instead, it is a sacred and divine institution that should be seen and respected as such. That's why the Christian marriage cannot thrive without God's presence and help—since He alone has the blueprint of how it is meant to work.

2. MARRIAGE IS HONOURABLE

Hebrews 13:4, reads **"Marriage is honourable among all..."** In other words, marriage is to be considered honourable by all people. Why? Because whatever comes from God is worthy of the honour His production bestows on it. If God is worthy of our honour, so is whatever He creates or establishes.

3. MARRIAGE IS A COVENANT

The world treats marriage as a contract between two people in love. But that's because they don't understand marriage. From God's perspective, marriage is a covenant between three parties. The **man**, the **woman** and their **God**. Yes, God is the third member of every Christian marriage. As a matter of fact, He is not just a member of the union, He is the Author, the Finisher, and the Foundation of it.

When you take your vows, you are not just making promises to your spouse, you are making that vow to your God as well. A contract usually contains clauses that allow you to nullify it. But a covenant is for life. Only death can nullify a covenant that's backed by an oath or a vow. A covenant is only made by one who intends to keep it—because it's a matter of integrity.

4. MARRIAGE IS A STEWARDSHIP

If you choose to get married, you have chosen to be a steward. A steward is someone who manages and looks after another person's property, wealth or business. In the same way, God designed your marriage to be the outworking of your commitment to take good care of your spouse. If you are not prepared to do so 'till death', you better stay single, because your spouse is God's property.

5. MARRIAGE IS A GIFT FROM GOD

You have to enter the marriage union knowing that it is a gift from God to you. I say that because not everyone who would like to get married gets to do so. Even if the marriage is not perfect, the fact that you've found someone to love (and someone who hopefully loves you back), is a blessing. When you see your marriage as a gift from God, you are more likely to treat it with the care and gratitude it deserves. It is that care and gratitude that attracts a better marriage experience.

6. MARRIAGE IS A TRANSFORMER

Be prepared to change when you get married, because God designed the marriage institution to change and mature you. Most people enter marriage, a little selfish and stuck in their ways. I know that because it happened to me! So the first few years of your marriage, will shape and reshape you into a mirror image of your spouse. If you resist that natural process of changing, your marriage will not make it.

7. MARRIAGE IS A MAGNIFIER

Marriage has a way of amplifying what is happening in your life—whether good or bad. When two people get as close and as connected as a husband and wife, they live with every flaw and fault every day. And it gets magnified. They also live with all the good stuff. But as most people are predisposed to being negative or critical, the bad stuff has a way of getting the best of us. Later in the course, I will try to help you anticipate this phenomenon, and show you how to avoid the mistakes most couples make, in the early parts of their marriage.

8. MARRIAGE IS GOOD FOR SOCIETY

Another amazing thing about marriage is that it is necessary for a well-functioning society. History proves again and again, that societies that devalue marriage and favour indiscriminate sexual orgies, usually implode within two or three generations. It happened in Sodom and Gomorra. It happened in Babylon, Egypt, Ancient Greece, and the Ancient Roman Empire. Conversely, nations and cultures that encourage and protect the marriage institutions tend to flourish. They have fewer problems with their children, less crime, less truancy, less gang culture, less incarceration and less waste of human potential—to mention a few.

9. MARRIAGE IS A MARATHON

Lastly, you have to remember that marriage is for life. That was God's original intention. That one man and one woman would love and support each other until death separates them. Truth be told, you can't do that if you treat your marriage as a sprint. But if you and your spouse decide to keep at it for the long haul, I promise you, you'll not regret it. I say that because, like good wine, marriage can get sweeter with age.

By the grace of God, I've enjoyed the last 19 years of marriage more than the first 19 years. It's amazing! Each time I think it can't get better, it does. That's what I want for you, as you prepare for this amazing life journey called marriage.

Prepare Yourself To Work At Your Marriage

Marriage is really hard work, but the benefits are amazing. So before you get married make sure you have the stamina and the tenacity to stay the course. To tell you the truth, I can't guarantee that there won't be days you wonder whether you made a mistake by getting married. There may be times you even question your choice of a partner.

It's all part of the marriage experience. It happens to every marriage to some degree or another. Conflict will happen when you least want it, and there will be plenty of misunderstandings too. Nevertheless, none of these things proves that you have a bad marriage. Instead, they simply prove that you are both fallen human beings—and that means you both need God's help.

If you've ever watch top class athletes, they prepare themselves physically and mentally for each event. They warm up, stretch and psych themselves up to perform optimally. Well, that's what you need to do before you get married. Understand that there are going to be some rough times as both of you learn to gel and compliment each other. Also remember that a good dose of patience and determination is what will see you through the rough times.

Recognise Your Expectations

Another thing you must evaluate and adjust is your expectations. Most people go into marriage with huge and unrealistic expectations. I'm not suggesting that you should not have desires, goals and dreams of the kind of marriage you want to build. I am suggesting, however, that it may take you more time to get there. And while you are journeying in that direction, you would need to be patient and realistic.

Just because you are in love doesn't mean that you will agree on everything. Just because you are in love doesn't mean that you would know how to complement each other. These things come with wisdom and time. That time may be longer or shorter depending on several things. For example, if you are both naturally stubborn, gelling together may take longer for you. Other issues that affect relational intimacy include, how mature you are, how yielded to God you are, and how attached you are to your ways of doing things.

The point is to temper your expectations because relationships are complicated. Understand that you are both on an adventure that may have uncomfortable twists and turns along the way. Remember that the goal is to stay on the journey, not to give up before you arrive. It will get better with time and as you both mature in marriage matters.

Make Sure You've Heard From God

When I was a teenager, I learnt a most valuable lesson. That lesson was not to start a romantic relationship with anyone without first praying about it. And it wasn't just the talking to God part, it was the hearing from God part that mattered the most. Those who taught us to do this also taught us to commit every area of our lives to God.

We were encouraged to speak to God about every little thing in our lives, because God is interested in everything we do. We were also encouraged to practice hearing God. The leader of the fellowship I attended said: "If you don't learn how to decipher God's will in the little things, you are not going to know His will when it comes to your decision on who to marry."

Well, that's exactly what I did. I prayed about starting a relationship with one lovely lady I was interested in, but sensed after a while that God was saying 'No' to the relationship. I didn't hear a loud voice or see a flashing light, but I knew that person wasn't His will for me. Something just didn't click, and I didn't have peace. That's how God usually speaks to me. If I don't have peace, I don't make huge decisions. Period!

My point is that marriage is too precious to embark upon without hearing from God. You need to know that your life partner is approved by your Lord and King. So, make sure your marriage desires are soaked in prayers. Ask for God's wisdom. Ask for discernment. And more importantly, ask for someone you can love and serve for the rest of your life.

Too many people ask God for shallow or immaterial things. They often have a list of shallow qualities they want in a spouse, so they can feel good about themselves. They pray prayers like: "Lord, give me a rich, tall and handsome guy. I want him to have a six-pack, drive a Tesla, and be very successful."

What if God answered your prayers and gave you everything on your list, but he didn't give you anything that you messed out of your list? So, let's say the guy who shows up is rich and good-looking, but he is also brutish and abusive. He has a six-pack and drives a Tesla, but he is a liar, a cheat, and a womaniser. What then?

Do you see why you can't just pray about what you want in a partner? You must also pray about what you don't want. You don't want a bully, a cheat, or a dishonest spouse. You don't want a liar, a thief, a serial abuser, or a child molester either.

So, make sure you've heard from the Lord. He loves you and only wants the best for you. But remember, nobody comes into your life as a finished product. Your future husband or wife would come with some flaws. He may not initially look like your dream prince in shining armour. And she may not look like your flawless and beautiful poster girl, either. What matters most is that he or she is God's precious gift to you—and you know it.

Understand That You Both Carry Baggage

As you prepare yourself for marriage, remember that the person you marry has a past. He or she had or has a family. They grew up in a community. They have a personality, a temperament, and a disposition. The same is true for you as well. You have a past, a personality, a temperament and a peculiar mindset that was formed by your personal experiences.

That means you will both need to patiently and lovingly labour together to become a unified whole. It's like trying to fit a square peg into a round hole. Some parts of you would have to give and some parts of your spouse would have to change too. Until you are both happy to evolve in several areas of life, your marriage will always be bumpy and painful.

For example, you or your partner may carry emotional scars from past relationships or experiences, which can affect your perception, behaviour or interactions within the marriage. I know of a couple who struggled with chronic trust issues because one partner had been betrayed in a previous relationship. That particular dynamic led to jealousy and extreme insecurity.

I knew of another couple who stopped communicating seriously altogether in their home, because it often led to tension and misunderstanding. One partner grew up in a household where expressing emotions was suppressed, while the other partner came from a family of noisy and passionate debaters.

My point is that we all picked up some baggage along the way. Some more than others. If you put in the effort to understand your spouse a little more, you would be slow to get angry or frustrated when you come across some of your partner's hard-core baggage. Instead, you will ask God to teach you patience, humility and empathy. After all, you have your baggage too!

Embrace The Reality Of The Marriage Covenant

Marriage is a Covenant that two people make with each other and with God, to live together as husband and wife for the rest of their lives. And to prove that marriage is really a Covenant, you and your spouse will agree on the terms of your Covenant and declare them to each other in front of God, your minister, your family, and your friends—in the form of vows.

Now a Covenant is an unbreakable promise made before God, to do what has been promised on demand. It is based on the integrity of the one who gave the promise and not on the performance or merit of the one receiving the promise. In other words, if I have a Covenant (or unbreakable promise) with you to look after your dog for the next 5 years, I am bound by that Covenant to do what I promised whether or not you do anything for me in return.

That's the nature of a Covenant. A contract on the other hand requires the two parties to perform their part as required, or the contract can be nullified. If you don't understand this important difference, you will always base your decision to serve and care for your spouse on his or her ability to serve and care for you.

A Covenant only requires one party to do what they promised. I will repeat that for emphasis: **A Covenant only requires one party to do what they promised.** That's why God doesn't have a contract with His children; He has a Covenant with us. When He promises to do something for us, He does it whether we deserve it or not. God still loves us when we fail Him. He cares for us when we dishonour Him. He blesses us when we disobey Him. That's how a Covenant works!

You do your part because you promised to do so. A Covenant helps you become a person of your word. It is an unconditional commitment to deliver on your promise. A Covenant doesn't change with the seasons or with the wind. It doesn't get discarded when one party is weak or discouraged.

That's why marriages don't work well outside of a Covenant agreement. When you say your marriage vows, you are sealing your Marriage Covenant. You are not just saying your vows to your spouse, or before family and friends; you are saying them before the God of heaven. Therefore, if you break the vows you made to your spouse, you are also breaking the vows you made to Almighty God.

Ecclesiastes 5: 4-5 says: **When you make a vow to God, do not delay to pay it; For He has no pleasure in fools. Pay what you have vowed. Better not to vow than to vow and not pay.**

When you understand that marriage is a Covenant, you will focus more on what you can do to maintain or strengthen that Covenant, than what your spouse is or isn't doing right.

Understand And Embrace The Five Stages Of Marriage

Your marriage will go through **five** predictable seasons, stages or phases if you stay in it through the ups and downs of your relationship journey. While these seasons may not have specific timeframes and can vary from couple to couple, they provide a fairly accurate framework for understanding the evolution and dynamics of marriage.

Here are five commonly recognised seasons of marriage. If you take them to heart, you will be better prepared to navigate them.

1.) The Season of Infatuation

This phase of the relationship is often referred to as the honeymoon phase. It's when everything feels new, exciting, and exhilarating. You are deeply infatuated with each other, and there is a sense of euphoria and a strong emotional connection. During this season, you may idealise each other, overlook your differences, and experience intense emotional and physical attraction. You may also find it easy to communicate; and conflicts may be minimal, as you both focus on enjoying the bliss of being in love. On average, this season typically lasts for 1 to 2 years.

2.) The Season of Adjustment

As the initial honeymoon phase fades, you will enter a period of adjustment. Some people call it the Power Struggle stage. This is when you begin to confront the realities of everyday life as a couple. Typically, this season is marked by a more thorough scrutiny of each other's habits, preferences, and idiosyncrasies. You are more likely to encounter challenges as you navigate differences in your expectations, your communication styles, and your deep-rooted habits. It's a time to learn how to negotiate, establish boundaries and master the **art** of conflict resolution. This will usually be a season of tension and disagreements, but it will also help to lay a foundation for building mutual understanding and trust in the years to come. Depending on how much adjustment is required in the marriage, this season of marriage can last for 4 to 6 years.

3.) The Season of Growth

In this third season of marriage, you will experience significant personal and relational growth. Your desire to overcome major obstacles and create a stable home for your children will make you more resilient. Your bond with your spouse would deepen, and you would learn to overcome obstacles and solve problems together. You will weather storms, face adversity and adapt to life's changes as a team. In this season, you will develop a greater sense of compassion, empathy, intimacy and appreciation for your partner. All things being equal, this season of growth should enable you to communicate and understand each other much better. Depending on how much growth and maturity is required in your situation, this season can last for the next 10 years.

4.) The Season of Stability

As you mature in your relationship, the next season of life is characterised by stability. You develop a deep sense of security, purpose and destiny. You learn to prioritise your relationship. You fight less frequently. You are more comfortable with each other. Your finances are normally a lot better, and you are able to share fulfilling milestones as a team. While challenges may still arise, you are better prepared to navigate them with confidence and resilience. This season can last for another 15-20 years.

5.) The Season of Reflection

In this final season of marriage, couples reflect on the journey they've travelled together. They get to appreciate the love they've shared, the lessons they've learnt, and the achievements they've experienced. They may even start to feel a renewed sense of gratitude for each other, for their children and grandchildren, and for all the wonderful memories they've shared. This is when they celebrate the legacy they've built together and reaffirm their commitment to each other and to the larger community of family and friends. Lastly, this season of reflection will normally provide them with opportunities to deepen their emotional intimacy, strengthen their love, and cultivate a greater sense of purpose for the years they have left.

COUPLES DISCUSSION POINTS

- What three important lessons have you learnt from this chapter? List them here.

  _____

  _____

  _____

- Which one of you is willing to take the lead in making sure that you constantly apply what you are learning to your relationship?

  _____

Your Premarital Journal

What thoughts, ideas, decisions and prayer points would you like to keep a record of after reading this part of the manual? Write them in the space below:

CHAPTER 7

HOW TO BUILD A SUCCESSFUL MARRIAGE

Two are better than one, because they have a good reward for their labour. (Ecclesiastes 4:9.)

Every marriage is different, and there are no one-size-fits-all solutions. What works in my marriage may not work in yours. Nevertheless, there are things common to nearly every marriage, because we are all humans with similar challenges and needs.

In this chapter, I will be taking you through my top **eleven** principles that help to build and strengthen Christian marriages. If you learn them diligently and apply them consistently to your life and marriage, you will be on your way to building an amazing foundation for a great future marriage.

PRINCIPLE #1

START WITH A CLEAR VISION FOR YOUR MARRIAGE

Where there is no vision, the people perish...

(Proverbs 29:18.)

If you want to build anything great, you need to build it on a clear and sensible vision. A definite vision is like a bridge. It takes you from where you are right now, to where you want to be or go. Vision is a clear picture of a better future that is well-defined and written down. Proverbs 29:18 says, **"Where there is no vision, the people perish..."**

Solomon was telling the people that vision is an important part of any significant endeavour. And, if people don't have a vision (of where they wish to go) they will stagnate and perish. This truism is key to any marriage endeavour as well. That's why you need to have a vision for your marriage.

What Your Vision Should Be Based On

It is one thing to have a written vision, but it is another thing to have a vision that is God-centred, love-based, and built on a motivation to serve your spouse. Most people's vision statements are unrealistic and selfishly motivated. For instance, it's unreasonable to hope for a marriage with no misunderstandings or with a spouse who is perfect in every way. That only happens on Pluto—not on Earth.

So, before you write out your **marriage vision statements**, it's important (first of all) to understand that you need to become the person who has what it takes to **achieve** that vision. In other words, you need to be willing to yield your will to God so He can change you into the person you need to be—that is someone who can carry the vision long-term and make it happen.

Are you willing to be that person? The one who can labour tirelessly with God's help—to develop the determination, tenacity and skills to make the vision a reality? If the answer to this question is 'yes', you have a 99% chance of actually achieving the vision. As a matter of fact, one of the benefits of having a clear vision is that it provokes personal growth—whether spiritual, emotional, psychological or relational.

How To Craft Your Marriage Vision

The best way to craft a well-defined marriage vision document is to start by discussing the ways you want your marriage to turn out in 5, 10 or 20 years. Start by discussing your answers to a set of questions, like the ones below.

1. What kind of marriage do we want to have?
2. What do we each want to get out of our marriage?
3. What values and ideals do we want to imbibe?
4. What outcomes will make us happy and content?
5. What are things we want to avoid in our marriage?

Be sure to take notes during your discussions. Note the words or phrases you both use to describe the type of marriage you want. Don't rush through this exercise, as it will help you develop a bond that can be priceless.

Below is an example of what your marriage vision statements might look like. Feel free to edit it, or use it as a template to develop your own unique version.

A Marriage Vision Document

Having discussed and prayed about the type of marriage we desire to have, _____ and _____, have agreed (by God's grace) to the following Vision statements for our marriage.

Date: _____

Signature: _____

Signature: _____

- We commit to being totally **faithful** and **loyal** to each other so that our marriage may enjoy a deep sense of trust and security.
- We will express our love **daily** through positive and uplifting words, loving touches and caring actions.
- We will make our home a place of open, honest, and respectful **communication** at all times.
- We will approach conflicts with **patience**, understanding and respect—and with a willingness to understand each other or resolve issues constructively.
- We will continue to build and maintain trust by being **transparent** and honest at all times.
- We vow to recognise each other's individuality, hear each other's opinions, and **respect** each other's boundaries, in all aspects of our relationship.

- We will endeavour to maintain **financial** stability and integrity by mutually agreeing on spending, giving and saving budgets.

- We commit to **grow** together spiritually, emotionally, mentally, relationally, professionally and personally. We will do this by creating quality time for continuous education, study and learning.

- We will **support** each other's dreams, ambitions, and personal goals.

- We will share family and household **responsibilities** fairly—and we will step in to support each other when it's right and loving to do so.

- We will nurture our physical, emotional and sexual intimacy, by keeping our relationship **passionate**, fun and vibrant.

- We will cultivate a strong marital **friendship** that allows us to enjoy each other's company, humour and laughter.

- We will explore new experiences and adventures together to create unforgettable **memories**.

- We will create time for **activities** that foster our physical, mental, and emotional well-being; and help us lead a healthy lifestyle.

- We will **practice** forgiveness intentionally, let go of past hurts, and learn to move forward with a clean slate.

- We will strive together to leave a positive **legacy** of love and forgiveness for our children and future generations.

A Clearly Defined Vision

Here are 10 things that a clearly defined vision will do for you and your marriage:

1.) **Purpose:** Having a meaningful vision gives your life purpose. It provides you and your partner with a definite sense of direction, aspiration, and passion in your daily activities and routines.

2.) **Decision-Making:** A clearly defined vision simplifies decision-making since you have a clear framework to evaluate your decisions and choices. Vision helps you to see whether the actions you are choosing to take are bringing you closer to your goals or not.

3.) **Resilience:** When you encounter obstacles, a strong vision helps you stay committed and resilient. That's usually because you have a compelling reason to stay the course instead of quitting.

4.) **Clarity:** A well-defined vision helps you understand what you want or don't want in your marriage; thus reducing uncertainty and ambivalence about what to do or what to avoid doing.

5.) **Overcoming Procrastination:** A strong vision reduces procrastination. When you have a compelling vision or reason to do something extraordinary with your life, you are more likely to take action.

6.) **Motivation:** Knowing what you want to achieve in your marriage relationship can be a powerful motivator. It keeps you focused, tenacious, and unwavering, especially when your relationship is faced with difficulties or conflict.

7.) **Growth:** Pursuing a well-defined vision often involves personal growth and development. As you labour to acquire the knowledge, skills and confidence required to achieve your vision, your capacity and aptitude increase, leading to personal and marital growth.

8.) **Direction:** A clear vision will provide your marriage with a reliable roadmap to where you are heading. It will also help you decide what steps you need to take to get there in one piece.

9.) **Creativity:** A well-defined vision fosters creativity as it forces you and your partner to explore innovative solutions or ways to reach your goals together.

10.) **Achievement:** Couples with a clear vision are more likely to set and achieve their marital goals since they have concrete ideas of what success would look like to them.

11.) **Satisfaction:** As you find yourself achieving major parts of your vision for your life or marriage, it will fill you with a deep sense of satisfaction and fulfilment.

12.) **Legacy:** A vision helps you think about the long-term impact you want to have on your children, family and community. This often helps to guide you towards actions that contribute to a meaningful life and a positive legacy for those looking up to you.

As you can see, having a clear and well-defined vision for your marriage is essential because it provides you with a long-term framework for success. It gives you direction and aids you in evaluating what you are doing to achieve your dreams.

How To Develop Your Marriage Vision

Many years ago, I used to love watching the Cosby Show because it was the closest thing to what I hoped my family life would look like. The way Bill Cosby and his wife (on set) related with their children reassured me that a beautiful, peaceful and loving home was possible.

Of course, it was only a television show, but that didn't matter to me. Every episode envisioned, empowered and gave me ideas for my future family. Best of all, the Cosby Show gave me a rough template of how to make it work.

I am not suggesting that you get the vision for your marriage from a television show; I am saying that you should find a way of etching a picture of what you want your marriage or family life to look like in your mind. In those early days of my life, the Cosby Show did that for me.

There are many other sources of a marital vision. For instance:

- Your vision can come from the wealth of Scriptures available to you in your Bible.

- You can get a vision from asking God to give you one and listening carefully to His reply.

- It can come from a beautiful family you know and admire or from the example of your parents or in-laws.

- You can get it from good Family Seminars and Workshops you attend.

- Or it can come from a well-written relationship book or an inspirational family movie.

The point is to make sure you have a vivid picture of what you desire your marriage to look like, and find a way to record and internalise it. If you are not married or don't have a marriage partner yet, you can do this exercise alone in anticipation of your preferred future. Ideally, the process works better if you have a partner to do the exercise with.

COUPLE'S HOMEWORK

- Some time this week, find time to sit down with your partner to write out a clear Vision Statement for your marriage. Make sure it includes whatever you see in your future.

- Which day have you chosen? _____

- Make some notes here: _____

_____

_____

_____

_____

_____

_____

_____

_____

_____

_____

_____

_____

Your Premarital Journal

What thoughts, ideas, decisions and prayer points would you like to keep a record of after reading this section and discussion it with your partner? Write them in the space below:

PRINCIPLE #2

UNDERSTAND YOUR DIFFERENCES

Then God saw everything that He had made, and indeed it was very good. So the evening and the morning were the sixth day. (Genesis 1:31.)

God created men and women to be different on many levels. This was by no means a mistake—but was at the centre of God's will for His creation. That's why immediately after God created mankind, He said, **"It is very good."** So, why did God create and wire men and women differently? What was His reason?

I believe God wired us differently for several important reasons. Here are some of them:

1. God wired us differently to perform different functions, responsibilities and roles. For instance, God designed a woman to breastfeed her children. So, she has a breast to perform that function. Similarly, God designed a man to procreate. So, He gave him a tool for that purpose also. My point is that design determines function. God made males and females differently because He intended for them to have different roles and responsibilities.

2. God wired us differently to make us attractive to each other. Six thousand years of human existence have shown us that we are generally attracted to what we lack. We are attracted to people who have what we don't have—but need. If a man wants a child, he is going to be attracted to a woman who can help him meet that need. And if a woman wants a traditional family, she is going to look for a man who can fulfil that deep heart desire. Only opposites can do that!

3. God wired us differently to make our lives more colourful, more intriguing, and more three-dimensional. Imagine how boring life would be if we all looked and behaved alike. As you look at creation, you can't fail to recognise that God is a God of variety. There are over fifteen thousand varieties of flowers alone.

And, there are numerous kinds of dogs, fish, insects, trees, and so on.

4. God wired us differently to complement each other. God made men and women to complement each other. We are like two sides of a pair of scissors. One half can't function effectively alone, it needs the other half. In the same way, marriage works well when we understand and appreciate these unique differences, instead of resisting them or trying to change them.

The key to navigating these differences is to realise them, accept them, and see them as assets in your relationship. I'll say that again for emphasis: **The differences between you and your partner are assets in your relationship, not liabilities.**

That's why the Bible says: **"In the same way, you husbands must give honour to your wives. Treat your wife with understanding as you live together. She may be weaker than you are, but she is your equal partner in God's gift of new life. Treat her as you should so your prayers will not be hindered."** (1 Peter 3:7.) NLT.

Notice, that the Bible encourages us to deal with each other from a place of understanding—or accurate knowledge. Why? Because what makes men tick, hardly ever has the same effect on women. We are totally different creatures—and are wired to see, think and function differently. I can tell you from experience, that one of the most constructive giant leaps in my marriage took place when I understood and embraced my wife's differences as necessary and needed assets in our relationship.

Let me say that again because it is that important. One of the most constructive relational leaps in my marriage, took place when I understood and embraced my wife's differences—as necessary and needed assets in our relationship.

Some Major Differences Between the Sexes

1. We Are Physically Different.

The most obvious differences between men and women are physical. Generally, men have more muscle mass, denser bones, and lower body fat than women. These differences are mainly due to hormones like testosterone in men and estrogen in women. For instance, men's bodies are typically better suited for activities that require strength and endurance, which is why they often excel in sports like weightlifting and sprinting. Women, on the other hand, usually have more body fat around the hips and thighs, which is important for reproduction. Additionally, because women have higher levels of estrogen and oxytocin, they are often more sensitive to emotional and social signals. This level of emotional sensitivity is beneficial in nurturing roles and professions that require empathy and good communication skills.

2. We Are Emotionally Different.

Women and men also differ in how they express and process emotions. Women tend to be more expressive with their emotions, often displaying them more openly too. This trait also makes women more communicative and empathetic. In contrast, men often suppress emotional expression and tend to display a more stoic demeanour. For example, in stressful situations, women would often seek social support and openly discuss their feelings, while men would often internalise their stress and adopt problem-solving paradigms.

3. We Communicate Differently.

Women typically use more words and nonverbal signals to convey their thoughts and feelings, which helps to foster deeper connections and clearer communication. Men, however, often communicate more directly and with fewer words. For example, in a workplace setting, women would often provide more context and detail in their communications, while men tend to be concise and abrupt in their communication methods. Women often elaborate on their points and use more collaborative language, while men might get straight to the point and use more assertive or authoritative language.

4. We Listen and Respond Differently.

Men and women also differ in their listening styles. Women are more likely to use active listening techniques, showing empathy and understanding through nodding and verbal affirmations. Men, on the other hand, often listen to solve problems and may interrupt more frequently to offer solutions. For instance, in a conversation about personal issues, a woman might listen attentively and offer emotional support, while a man might quickly suggest practical solutions. These differing approaches can sometimes lead to frustration if not understood and appreciated by both parties.

5. We Process Information Differently.

Men and women think and process information differently because of subtle differences in their brain structure. Men usually have larger brains with more grey matter. This helps them with tasks that require high spatial coordination—like reading maps and building systems. Women, on the other hand, have more white matter and neurons in the areas of the brain that help with communication and emotions. This helps them to talk and multitask better. When solving problems, men often break problems down into parts and tend to think logically, while women look at the whole picture and consider many factors. Men and women also respond to stress differently. Men often have a "fight or flight" response, which means they get ready to either face the problem or run away. Women tend to seek support from friends and family, thanks to the "tend and befriend" response they utilise better.

6. We Socialise and Interact Differently.

Social interaction styles also differ between the genders. Women often prioritize building and maintaining relationships. That's because they show more collaborative and cooperative behaviour. Men, however, tend to engage in more competitive and hierarchical behaviour. In the workplace settings, women usually try to include everyone's ideas and get everyone to agree, while men often show their authority or challenge others to prove their position.

7. We have Different Spiritual and Ethical Perspectives.

There are also differences in spiritual and ethical perspectives between men and women. Research and surveys suggest that women are generally more spiritual or ethereal than men. Women engage in and enjoy religious activities and practices more than men. This may be linked to women's roles in nurturing and community-building, which align with many religious and spiritual values. This spiritual inclination contributes to their sense of purpose and well-being. Men, on the other hand, tend to engage more in combative or adrenaline-fueled activities, like boxing or racing cars. Even when men are spiritually inclined, they tend to be less emotionally engaged.

Conclusion

I think it is safe to say that one of the reasons we deal with things differently is because we have different roles and responsibilities. If we embrace these differences, they will enrich our collective human experience. They will foster greater cooperation and empathy between men and women; and put us in a better position to work proactively together in marriage. That's why it's so important to see these differences in our partners as assets and not liabilities.

Your Premarital Journal

Did this section help you better understand some aspects of your partner's attitude or behaviour? Discuss it together.

- How will this knowledge affect your attitude and actions in the future?
- What decisions and prayer points would you like to record in the space below?

PRINCIPLE #3

LEARN TO NAVIGATE CONFLICT

Make allowance for each other's faults, and forgive anyone who offends you. Remember, the Lord forgave you, so you must forgive others. (Colossians 3:13.) NLT.

I like to define conflict as a serious misunderstanding or disagreement that leads to clashes, quarrels, or fights with another person or party. Conflict is an inevitable part of marriage. It comes with the territory and cannot be avoided, escaped, or prayed away. However, you can learn to navigate it appropriately with minimal disruption.

Ironically, nothing can help you grow in marriage more than conflict. Conflict can either soften or harden your heart, depending on your heart's condition. But if you allow God to guide you, He can use conflicts to make you more Christlike—by teaching you to handle situations in a way that honours Him and your spouse.

In Romans 12:17-21, Paul instructs us to:

> **"Repay no one evil for evil. Have regard for good things in the sight of all men. If it is possible, as much as depends on you, live peaceably with all men. Beloved, do not avenge yourselves, but rather give place to wrath; for it is written, 'Vengeance is Mine, I will repay,' says the Lord. Therefore 'If your enemy is hungry, feed him; If he is thirsty, give him a drink; for in so doing you will heap coals of fire on his head.' Do not be overcome by evil, but overcome evil with good."**

Considering that we are called to live like this with friends and neighbours, how much more should we strive to live like this with our spouses?

Here are more truths about conflict:

1. **Conflict is the result of differences:** Men and women are profoundly different. They are wired differently, think and process information differently, and have different preferences and appetites.

2. **Conflict is the consequence of our selfish and self-centred behaviour:** We fight because our egos often get in the way of dealing maturely and sensitively with issues.

3. **Conflict is the product of our brokenness:** Our old sinful nature tends to emerge when we least expect it, and results in avoidable conflict.

The problem is not that we have conflict, but that we don't know how to handle it biblically and maturely. We don't know how to fight fair. We don't know how to apologize, how to forgive, and how to make up quickly.

When I was courting my wife, I often wondered why we were not taught how to resolve our quarrels or conflicts in a spouse-honoring way. I spent over 20 years in school, but never once did we have any conflict resolution lessons. Isn't that crazy, considering that conflict is common to every relationship? Why didn't anyone think it would be an excellent idea to include conflict resolution in our educational curriculum? I suppose I'll never know!

How To Handle Conflict Effectively

There are several effective ways to handle conflict—or what I like to call, 'learning to fight fairly'. Since we know that conflict is inevitable in every relationship, our goal should be to limit the damage it can cause in the marriage.

It's possible to quarrel about an issue, and yet both parties can leave the discussion with a better understanding of their partner—instead of a bitter experience. That's what I mean by 'fighting fairly'.

How To Fight Fairly

Learning to fight fairly in a marriage means addressing conflicts and disagreements in a constructive, respectful and healthy manner. It's about communicating effectively and resolving issues without causing harm to each other or the relationship. This approach ensures that each partner feels heard, understood, and valued, even during disagreements. It involves maintaining a sense of empathy, patience, and a willingness to see the other person's perspective.

Here are some key principles and practical examples to help **couples** fight fairly, ensuring that conflicts become opportunities for growth rather than sources of ongoing strife:

1. Stay Focused on the Issue at Hand.

It is easy to start a discussion about one issue and end up fighting over another. That's why you must learn to focus on one issue at a time. Avoid bringing up unrelated issues or historical grievances. For example, if you're arguing about finances, don't abruptly bring up a concern you had about your partner's sister. Stick to one topic until it is resolved before moving on to another issue.

2. Avoid Personal Attacks:

Too often, when there is conflict over an issue, the discussion can get super personal. You start to attack each other's character or motivations. Or you may resort to disrespectful language, name-calling or insults. That is never profitable. Instead of saying, "You always ignore me!" or "You never come home on time."—which may sound like a personal attack on your spouse; say, "I feel neglected when we don't have time for each other." or "I don't enjoy not knowing when you would be home."

3. Employ Active Listening:

Active listening requires that you listen to your partner intently without interrupting. It also requires you to show from your response that you have understood their viewpoint. You can do that by making eye contact when your partner is speaking or nodding to show you're paying attention. Also, it is good practice to confirm what you've heard by making statements like, "Are you saying that...?" or "I think I hear you saying that..." This allows your partner to correct your interpretation of their concern, or acknowledge that you are on the right path.

4. Seek to Understand, Not to Win the Argument:

Aim for mutual understanding and resolution rather than trying to win the argument. Instead of trying to prove your point at all costs, ask questions like "Can you help me understand why you feel this way?" or "I think I'm right, but why do you think I'm wrong?". Questions like this help to foster understanding and empathy.

5. Use "I" Statements:

Express your feelings and thoughts without blaming your partner. Instead of saying, "You never listen to me," say, "I feel unheard when you don't look at me while I'm speaking." "I" statements reduce your partner's tendency to be defensive, and it creates space for a more productive dialogue.

6. Take a Timeout if Needed:

Sometimes the best thing to do during a heated argument is to call a timeout. Just signal to your partner that you'd like to pause the discussion to calm down and gather your thoughts. Agree on a set time to process the situation (say, 15 or 20 minutes), and then return to the discussion—hopefully with a better perspective or a more measured approach. This reduces escalation and allows for clearer thinking.

7. Work Towards a Compromise:

Compromise is not a dirty word when it comes to marriage. As a matter of fact, it is essential. In many cases, you would need to find a middle ground where you both can feel that your needs are met. Agree to each express your ideal outcome and then look for a solution that satisfies both of you. But for that to work, you must be willing to give a little—to get a little.

8. Be quick to Apologize or Forgive:

It's impossible for two people to live together without hurting each other at some point. But sincerely saying sorry when you've hurt your partner and being willing to forgive when you've been hurt, is the key to marital harmony. So learn to acknowledge your mistakes without making excuses. Also, express your willingness to forgive when your partner is truly sorry. But don't expect perfection, because it's unreasonable.

Additional Tips

- **Set Ground Rules:** Agree on rules for fair fighting, such as no shouting or name-calling.
- **Choose the Right Time and Place:** Avoid discussing serious issues when either partner is tired, hungry, or stressed.
- **Use Humor if appropriate:** Sometimes, humour can defuse tension and bring perspective.
- **Seek Professional Help if Needed:** A counsellor or therapist can provide tools and strategies for healthy conflict resolution.

Learning to 'fight fairly' ensures that conflicts become opportunities for marital growth and deeper understanding, instead of sources of resentment, anger and bitterness. By adopting some of the ideas above, you will handle disagreements in a way that strengthens your relationship and endears your partner to you.

To fight fairly you and your spouse must be willing to embrace four important **convictions** and four important **ground rules**.

THE FOUR CONVICTIONS

Conviction #1:

You are dealing with a Precious Child of God.

If you and your partner are Bible-believing believers, you know that you are both children of the Most High God. God is your Father and Jesus is your brother. That means your partner is God's precious son or daughter. So you need to be very careful when you are dealing with this precious child of God—because your spouse is the apple of His eyes. And, he or she is very precious in God's sight.

Conviction #2:
You and your Spouse are on the same side.

The next conviction I want you to embrace as you learn to fight fairly is that you and your spouse are heirs of the grace of life. That means you are both in this life together and on the same team. Too often, couples forget this powerful reality in the sandstorm of their conflicts. So, do whatever you can to remember that you are one flesh—and that God wants you to move in the same direction.

Conviction #3:
You have a common Enemy.

Try not to be shortsighted. Your spouse is not your enemy. Even if your spouse does something to really hurt you, you must understand that your real enemy is Satan. He is the instigator, the liar and the accuser. He will use anyone and anything he can find to harm you. So don't be ignorant of his devices. Your spouse is not your enemy, Satan is.

Conviction #4:
God anticipated every Challenge you would face and promised to provide a Solution.

The fourth conviction that will help you fight fairly is understanding and believing that none of your challenges took God by surprise. God is Omniscient. That means He knows everything. He knew the challenges you would face before you were even born. Being a good God, He went ahead of you to supply everything you'd ever need to withstand, solve, or overcome them.

Paul talked about God's all-knowing Wisdom when he wrote:

> **No temptation has overtaken you except such as is common to man; but God is faithful, who will not allow you to be tempted beyond what you are able, but with the temptation will also make the way of escape, that you may be able to bear it.** (1 Corinthians 10:13.)

The Greek word translated 'temptation' also means provocation, trials or setbacks. The most amazing part of this reassurance from God's Word is that He limits that test and trials, to the degree He knows we can safely handle.

Whenever you remember and practice these four convictions, it will become much easier to respond to conflict in a **God-honouring** and **spouse-honouring** manner.

To fight fairly you must also be willing to embrace **four** ground rules too.

THE FOUR GROUND RULES

Ground Rule #1

I will approach every Conflict with the desire to Reconcile.

In Matthew 5:23-24, Jesus said, **"Therefore if you bring your gift to the altar, and there remember that your brother has something against you, leave your gift there before the altar, and go your way. First be reconciled to your brother, and then come and offer your gift."**

Always remember that the goal of conflict resolution is to resolve the conflict amicably—not to be right, to win the argument, or to humiliate your spouse. So, approach every conflict with a desire to reconcile. If this is your sincere heart's desire, you will find that it will help you listen to understand your spouse better, and it will help you reduce any tendency to make a mountain out of a molehill.

Ground Rule #2

Every conflict must lead to an Apology and Forgiveness.

In Luke 17:3-4, Jesus gave us another rule. This time He said, **"Take heed to yourselves. If your brother sins against you, rebuke him; and if he repents, forgive him. And if he sins against you seven times in a day, and seven times in a day returns to you, saying, 'I repent,' you shall forgive him."**

The next rule that helps to resolve conflict has to do with **apologies** and **forgiveness**. For conflict to be resolved properly, at least one party must be willing to apologise and the other must be willing to forgive. Sometimes, both parties need to apologise for something and forgive each other for something else. The only question you need to ask yourself is: **"Which one of the two, do I owe my spouse?"**

Ground Rule #3

It's okay to be Upset, but it is not okay to Sin.

The third ground rule to remember when you are trying to resolve a conflict is that: "It's okay to be upset, but it is not okay to sin." Getting upset or angry is natural, but sinning is optional. When some people are upset they think it's okay to insult, abuse or get physical with their spouse, but it's not okay. In Ephesians 4:26, Paul says, **"Be angry, and do not sin."** The Bible recognises that 'anger' is sometimes appropriate, but it never condones sin. Why? Because sin devalues and demeans. It humiliates and it gives Satan a foothold in your life. And you don't want that.

Ground Rule #4

I will listen to Understand my spouse's Heart— not just his or her Words.

Sometimes your spouse may be talking about one frustration, but that may just be the tip of the iceberg. This ground rule encourages you to listen out for the **heart** of the problem. For instance, your spouse may act out of character or make a big fuss over something that seems insignificant at the time. Well, listen out for the real cause or what triggered that kind of reaction. Could your spouse be feeling insecure, abandoned or jealous? The better you understand why your spouse is upset, the quicker you can make the necessary adjustments or corrections.

If these four Convictions and four Ground Rules are practised intentionally, they can become a powerful framework for conflict resolution and reconciliation in all your relationships.

My Personal Advice

I usually advise couples to print out the **four Convictions** and the **four Ground rules**, frame them and place them where they can easily access and ponder on the process before attempting to discuss any conflict that may arise. When couples do that, they are reminded of these principles and are less likely to make things worse.

Next, you need a Strategy

The next stage of the process is to use this strategy I developed to smoothen the process of resolving conflict. The process can always be adjusted or finetuned to suit your personality or way of life.

1.) Choose the right time and place to resolve your conflicts.

Immediately after a conflict arises is not usually the right time to resolve it. Why? Because tempers are usually still high. Adrenaline is in full flow, and you are usually still furious over what happened. So my advice to you is to take a meditation break.

What is a Meditation Break?

A meditation break is an opportunity you give yourself to go for a short walk or to your thinking corner, to think about what's really upsetting you and what you can do to resolve it in a God-honouring manner. You can go to your study, bedroom, local library or café. What matters is that you give yourself this time to think or process your feelings, calm down, and go back with a strategy to make things better.

This step is crucial because:

a.) The best time to deal with conflict is when you've **calmed down** and put things into perspective. It's amazing how what looked like an immovable mountain can turn out to be a stepping stone to better understanding, once the dust settles.

b.) The best time to deal with conflict is when you've **identified** the real problem. In other words, the issue at hand isn't fuzzy, but clear to you. For instance, it's very easy to think that the problem is the person, when 90% of the time, the problem is not the person, but some misunderstanding or miscommunication.

c.) The best time to deal with conflict is when you've prayed for **wisdom** to deal with it in a godly way, and you feel you have the wisdom and composure to do so.

This is why the Bible teaches us to, **"be swift to hear, slow to speak, slow to wrath; for the wrath of man does not produce the righteousness of God."** (James 1:19-20.)

Once the aggrieved person has **processed** the heart of the issue, the next step is to:

2.) Remind yourself of the four Convictions and four Ground rules.

The four Convictions are:

1.) My spouse is a precious child of God.

2.) My spouse and I are on the same side.

3.) We have only one enemy and his name is Satan.

4.) God anticipated we would have this kind of challenge and has provided a way of escape (that is, a way to solve it amicably.)

The four Ground Rules are:

1.) I will approach this conflict with the desire to reconcile—not to be right, to win the argument, or to humiliate my spouse.

2.) This conflict will lead to an apology and forgiveness.

3.) I might be upset, but it's not okay to sin against God or my spouse.

4.) I will listen to understand my spouse's heart—since there are always two sides to every conflict or story.

To be sure, going through this process takes a lot of **humility** and **discipline**, but it works. So I encourage you to use it.

After meditating and ruminating on the issue that caused the conflict, how best to deal with it, and the 4 Convictions and Ground rules, it's time to discuss the situation with your spouse.

3.) Schedule a time to talk—preferably that same day.

It's never a good idea to leave conflict to simmer because it allows the problem to fester and grow in the meantime. Yes, it's okay to take a minute to think or get yourself together, but it's unwise to leave things for too long. That's why the Bible commands us not to go to bed angry.

> **"Be angry and do not sin; do not let the sun go down on your anger, and give no opportunity to the devil."** (Ephesians 4:26-27.)

Notice the reason Paul gives for this instruction. It's to stop Satan from taking advantage of the situation, to muddle the waters and to make things worse in your home.

Minimise Distraction

When you do sit down to discuss, agree to minimise interruption. That means no kids, no phones, no television, and no distraction. If either of you is very tired, you may need to agree to postpone the discussion for a while, but no more than 24 hours—if at all possible.

Remember that the goal of this discussion is to understand and restore harmony in the relationship. So, it's always wise to state this positive intention. You may also want to check if your spouse has had time to go through the four convictions and four ground rules. That's always the best place to start.

4.) When you start talking, follow these 5 steps.

1.) The person aggrieved should start the conversation with something positive—like 'how much you love, cherish, admire or respect your spouse'. You should do this because it helps to break the ice and **softens** the heart of both you and your partner. It also helps to set the tone for the rest of the discussion.

2.) The person aggrieved should remind their spouse that they are committed to the four Convictions and the four Ground rules. Why? Because you've both agreed at some point in the past, to resolve your conflicts using this method.

3.) Let your spouse know what you believe has happened, and especially how it made you feel. Remember that this is your view and your feelings only. As much as they are true for you, your spouse may not see or interpret the situation the same way. So be patient to hear their points too.

I suggest that you don't take more than **7 minutes** to complete this first part of the discussion. The reason is that if it goes on for too long, your partner may feel overwhelmed and simply switch off. In my opinion, men tend to be less patient when their wives appear to be giving them a 45-minute **lecture** after a conflict. So keep it brief and concise, except your spouse wants you to elaborate.

4.) After calmly sharing your thoughts and feelings, ask whether your spouse has understood your explanation. One way to do that is to ask if he or she would be willing to repeat what you've said back to you. That's another reason to keep your initial discussion short and to the point. From experience, about **50%** of the time, the conflict will be resolved here with a sincere apology, and hopefully, your forgiveness. The best resolutions happen when you both **see** where you could have dealt with the situation differently—and both apologise for the part you each played. Even if you think your contribution to the quarrel is only 1%. Apologise for the 1%.

5.) The other **50%** of the time, be willing to hear the other side of the story. As mentioned earlier, there are always two sides to any conflict, and both sides will often have some **valid** points. Remember the goal is to seek to understand, so you can empathise with your spouse. Don't be quick to negate the other person's viewpoints, since that might escalate the conflict and not serve you.

By all means, go back and forth a couple of times to try to understand your spouse, but don't dismiss their thoughts or feelings. If the conflict starts getting nasty, call for another meditation break, but agree to come back to it later—again not more than 24 hours. When you do get back, restart the process afresh.

Practical Tips

Here are **four** more practical tips to think about while trying to resolve conflict:

1.) Be open to the possibility that you may be wrong.

None of us is perfect, so even though we like to think that we are always right, the truth is that we are not. You are not a mind-reader. You are not all-knowing, and you are certainly not God. That said, you must always remember that the way you see or interpret something may be mistaken.

For several years of my marriage, I didn't understand this principle until I came to realise that, firstly, my memory wasn't always as reliable as I thought it was—and secondly, my hearing sometimes played tricks on me. At one point, I came up with this 'Twilight-Zone' concept: **"That between my wife's mouth and my ears, sounds get distorted."**

My point is that sometimes, our personality and our active imagination can skew what we see, hear or imagine. When that happens, you can argue until you are blue in the face, because you believe you saw, heard or imagined perfectly. Again the truth is that you don't always perceive things the way they are—because of your unique biology, psychology and experiences.

Never forget that we are all broken people, in a broken world ruled by evil spirits. We are all in the process of being healed and restored. Thus, make plenty of space for mistakes and misunderstandings. Mistakes in communication! Mistakes in intention! Mistakes in perception! And mistakes in actions taken!

Life Lessons:

Once you understand and acknowledge the reality of this **truism** above, you will do what I have learnt to do now. I have learnt to say certain things to my wife that have helped to reduce our conflicts drastically.

I have learnt to say statements like:

> "**I think I am right, but I may just be wrong.**" Or

> "**I thought I heard you say** (Whatever I thought I heard her say...) **– but I may have imagined it. I apologise.**" Or

> "**If that's what I said, I am really sorry. I meant to say...** (Whatever it was that I meant to say...)" Or

> "**I'm sorry if I communicated the wrong thing to you, but I meant to say...** (Whatever it was that I meant to say...)"

Statements like these are so **powerful** because they stop arguments and accusations dead in their tracks. But more than that, they show that you are **self-aware** and that you know you are not infallible.

1 John 1:10 says, **"If we say that we have not sinned, we make Him a liar, and His word is not in us.**

The previous verse says, **"If we confess our sins, He is faithful and just to forgive us our sins and to cleanse us from all unrighteousness."**

I'd like you to place your hand on your heart and make the following confession with me:

> Say, **"From today, I will be open to the fact that I may sometimes be wrong—because I'm not God."**

Say it again! And again!! And again!!!

2.) Choose being kind, over being right.

When it comes to relationships, being right is overrated. Being kind is far better. People remember when you are kind, but quickly forget when you are right. When I use the word 'right', I do not mean truth. We must always desire to be truthful. What I'm talking about is trying to prove your superiority without caring about your partner's feelings.

So it's possible to win the **battle** of who's right—but lose the **war** of who's kind. Endeavour to be kind in every conflict because the goal is to reconcile, not to prove you are better, or humiliate your spouse.

A story that cemented this principle for me is of the woman caught in the act of adultery in John chapter 8. While Jesus was teaching one day, a squad of Scribes and Pharisees dragged a terrified woman to Jesus. They wanted to see whether Jesus would keep the letter of the law or not.

"This woman was caught in the very art of adultery", they said, "and we think she should be stoned according to the Torah. In their mind, they were applying the Old Testament rules to the letter. They were right in their own eyes! She should be stoned. She deserved it for breaking the law.

Well, even if that was true and they were right, they were certainly not kind about it. Just think about this scenario for a minute: A married man was having sex with this woman when a mob of angry men rushed into the room. They grabbed the woman and gave the man a pass, but somehow reasoned that the woman alone deserved to be stoned.

Jesus on the other hand, was kind. He saw their hypocrisy and their hardness of heart—and wrote something mysterious on the ground. What He wrote was so convicting, that none of the Bible writers recorded what it was. Nevertheless, we know that His actions put the Scribes and Pharisees to shame and saved the woman's life.

What I'm trying to say is that the leaders of the Jews were technically 'right' to demand that the woman be stoned—going by the letter of the law. But Jesus was merciful and kind. I often tell people that being right doesn't stop you from getting a divorce, but being kind does.

The proud may be right, but the righteous are always kind. My point is that 'Kindness trumps 'rightness' every time.' I would rather be 'wrong' and stay married, than right and divorced.

3.) Be willing to suffer wrong for the sake of peace.

In 1 Corinthians 6, Paul addressed certain Christians who were offended, because they were dragging each other to court. Paul challenged them to be more Christlike, by choosing to suffer wrong instead of taking their fellow Christians to court. This is what he said to them:

"If any of you has a dispute with another, do you dare to

take it before the ungodly for judgment instead of before the Lord's people? Or do you not know that the Lord's people will judge the world? And if you are to judge the world, are you not competent to judge trivial cases? Do you not know that we will judge angels? How much more the things of this life!"

"The very fact that you have lawsuits among you means you have been completely defeated already. Why not rather be wronged? Why not rather be cheated? Instead, you yourselves cheat and do wrong, and you do this to your brothers and sisters." (1 Corinthians 6:1-3 & 7-8.) NIV.

The principle Paul was teaching us here is to be willing to forgive and suffer wrong—especially if the wrong that was done, was done by a believer. Well, if God expects us to forgive our fellow believers, how much more should we be willing to forgive our husband or wife? How much more should we be willing to suffer wrong sometimes?

Do you always have to be right? Do you have to win every conflict? Do you have to squash and humiliate your spouse? I don't think so. So learn to turn some things over to God. Learn to absorb the pain or the unfairness so that peace can reign. Learn to turn it over to God, because He promised to handle every injustice at the right time.

"Repay no one evil for evil, but give thought to do what is honourable in the sight of all. If possible, so far as it depends on you, live peaceably with everyone. Beloved, never avenge yourselves, but leave it to the wrath of God, for it is written, "Vengeance is mine, I will repay, says the Lord." (Romans 12:17-19.) ESV.

That's what Isaac did in Genesis 26. The Philistines envied him, quarrelled with him, and filled his wells with sand because they were jealous of his God-given success. Did he fight with them? Did he retaliate? Did he rein down curses on them? No, he didn't!

He simply walked away from the injustice that was done to him. Well, it wasn't long before God stopped the injustice and promoted him in the land. That is what you stand to **gain** when you let God fight your battles for you. This works in marriage as well.

And Isaac moved from there and dug another well, and

they did not quarrel over it. So he called its name Rehoboth, because he said, "For now the LORD has made room for us, and we shall be fruitful in the land.

(Genesis 26:22.)

Even Jesus was willing to suffer wrong. The Bible says: **"He was oppressed and He was afflicted, Yet He opened not His mouth; He was led as a lamb to the slaughter, And as a sheep, before its shearer is silent, so He opened not His mouth."** (Isaiah 53:7.)

So, be willing to suffer wrong because you know that no one is perfect. Be willing to suffer wrong for the sake of peace. If you do, it will teach you humility and activate God's promises for you.

4.) Try to visualise Conflict in the light of Eternity.

Conflict is best resolved when we approach it with two important things in mind. The first is **Eternity** and the second is **God's glory.** When you and your spouse are going through seasons of hurt and conflict, learn to ask yourself these two questions.

Question 1: **How important is what I am fighting about, in the light of eternity?**

Asking this question will help you put things into perspective. A dirty room, the toilet seat left open, the toothpaste pressed in the middle of the tube, or the fact that your hobby forgot to do the shopping—will always look trivial in the light of eternity.

Question 2: **How can I resolve this situation, so that in the end God is glorified?**

So much of what we do to each other in our relationships reflects badly on the God we represent and love. But that's because we generally don't think deeply enough about how some of our actions tarnish the glory of God. If we did, we would never act in such ways. This is why this second question is important as well.

All Conflict is Solvable

Finally, I want you to know that conflict is solvable—by the grace of God. You have to know deep within your heart that there is always a viable solution or a way to resolve any conflict you encounter. You just have to look for the solution passionately and creatively. I can say this confidently because God promised to give us a way to escape any test or trial we encounter.

> **"No temptation *(test, trial or calamity)* has overtaken you except what is common to mankind. And God is faithful; he will not let you be tempted beyond what you can bear. But when you are tempted, he will also provide a way out so that you can endure it".** (1 Corinthians 10:13.)

> Jesus said, **"If you can believe, all things are possible to the person who believes."** (Mark 9:23.)

> **"If any of you lacks wisdom, let him ask of God, who gives to all liberally and without reproach, and it will be given to him. But let him ask in faith, with no doubting, for he who doubts is like a wave of the sea driven and tossed by the wind…"** (James 1:5-6.)

So, when you go through challenges and conflict in your marriage, look for solutions and don't quit. There is always a way out—because every conflict is solvable! I'll say that again: **I'm convinced that every conflict is solvable.**

> **"Do not be anxious about anything, but in everything by prayer and supplication with thanksgiving let your requests be made known to God. And the peace of God, which surpasses all understanding, will guard your hearts and your minds in Christ Jesus."** (Philippians 4:6-7.)

Value peace highly and become a Peacemaker. Why? Because in a world filled with so much conflict, being a Peacemaker makes you very attractive. In addition, becoming a Peacemaker endears you to your spouse and reduces stress in your life. It improves your relationship and lightens the atmosphere in your home. It makes your relationships more fulfilling, and God is glorified in you.

Jesus said, **"Blessed are the peacemakers, for they shall be called sons of God."** (Matthew 5:9.)

The Prophet Isaiah said, "**The work of righteousness will be peace, And the effect of righteousness, quietness and assurance forever.**" (Isaiah 32:17.)

COUPLES DISCUSSION POINTS

- What new thing have you learnt about how to handle conflict effectively?

  _____

  _____

- What have you learnt about fighting fairly?

  _____

  _____

- Can you see the Conflict Resolution Strategy I share with you (in this chapter) working in your relationship?

  _____

  _____

- What can you do to help you remember the 4 Convictions, 4 Ground Rules, and the Strategy steps going forward?

  _____

  _____

Your Premarital Journal

What thoughts, ideas, decisions and prayer points would you like to keep a record of after reading this part of the manual? Write them in the space below:

PRINCIPLE #4

STRATEGIES FOR GOOD COMMUNICATION

"The single biggest problem in communication is the illusion that it has taken place." —George Bernard Shaw

Communication is a vital tool for sharing thoughts, concerns, and dreams with loved ones. It's the lifeline of any relationship and it is the bridge that connects your heart to the heart of the one you love. While communication can make you vulnerable, it's essential for the growth and harmony of the relationship.

A lack of positive or encouraging communication often signals trouble in a marriage. However, you can avoid this by learning how to communicate positively and by understanding the crucial communication differences between you and your partner. When communication in a marriage is healthy, the marriage is healthy too.

Let's examine some foundational precepts that you'll need to know as you learn to increase your ability to communicate better with your spouse.

1.) Remember that Communication does not end with talking.

The circle of good communication covers talking, listening, understanding and acting on what was communicated. Just because you've said something important doesn't mean that you effectively communicated with the intended recipient.

Several years ago, while I was doing some shopping in Italy, a seller was passionately trying to tell me something, but I didn't understand a word of what he was saying. He was speaking a language I didn't understand. He was talking; he was passionate; he was animated; but he was not communicating.

The same is true in marriage. Your spouse may hear what you said, but not interpret it the way you meant it. That's why it is important to check that your spouse is on the same page with you during any serious discussion.

One way to do this is to respectfully ask your spouse to repeat to you—in his or her own words—what they believe you've been saying. That way, you will be able to correct any misunderstanding and affirm whether your communication was successful or not.

2.) Understand that Communication is not a Science; it's an Art.

The way you communicate is a composite of your upbringing, your training, your conditioning, your personality, your body language and your language comprehension. And, none of these elements are the same for any two people. That's perhaps the reason why we often struggle to understand others.

Therefore, it's important to realise that good communication with your spouse will not happen overnight. Even after 39 years of marriage, my wife and I continually work on the way we communicate. The truth is that I am changing all the time, and so is she. So we keep learning and adapting and forgiving each other when we miss it because we are committed to communicating in a healthy and God-honouring way.

For we all make many mistakes, and if anyone makes no mistakes in what he says he is a perfect man, able to bridle the whole body also. (James 3:2.)

The point here is that communication is complex, and the results can be very unpredictable. Nevertheless, you can get better at communicating with time, even if you never quite hit perfection.

3.) Continuous Miscommunication will Eventually Lead to Severe Consequences.

I cannot count how many times my wife and I have said things to each other only to find out later, that a miscommunication had occurred. Usually, these incidents lead to hurtful and painful consequences. Sometimes they lead to tears, frustration or even anger.

The reason for this is simple. Words are powerful. They can build and they can destroy. They can encourage and they can discourage. They have the power to heal or to wound. That's why you cannot afford to be careless with your words. The Bible puts this truth like this:

> **The tongue is a small thing, but what enormous damage it can do. A tiny spark can set a great forest on fire. And the tongue is a flame of fire. It is full of wickedness that can ruin your whole life. It can turn the entire course of your life into a blazing flame of destruction, for it is set on fire by hell itself. People can tame all kinds of animals and birds and reptiles and fish, but no one can tame the tongue. It is an uncontrollable evil, full of deadly poison. Sometimes it praises our Lord and Father, and sometimes it breaks out into curses against those who have been made in the image of God.** (James 3:5-9. NLT.)

The Role of Effective Communication in Maintaining a Healthy Marriage.

Effective communication is vital in maintaining a healthy marriage, as it fosters understanding, trust, and emotional intimacy between you and your partner. By sharing your thoughts, feelings, and concerns openly, you can resolve conflicts better and build a stronger connection. When you communicate clearly and positively, you boost your partner's self-esteem and ensure that both of you feel valued and heard.

Good communication prevents misunderstandings and reduces the chances of resentment and anger. It creates a nurturing environment for love and respect to thrive. Good communication helps you make allowances for each other's differences and work together as a team. This ultimately strengthens your bond and contributes to long-term relationship satisfaction.

NINE GREAT COMMUNICATION STRATEGIES

#1. Develop the ability to Listen Actively

The goal of active listening is to really hear and understand your spouse. One way to make sure that you are actively practising reflective listening is to repeat what your spouse says back to them—which helps to confirm what you have understood. For instance, if your spouse mentions feeling overwhelmed at work, you may respond with a statement like: "It sounds like you're really being stressed at work." This not only shows that you've heard your spouse, but that you empathise with them too.

#2. Watch out for Non-Verbal Communication

Experts argue that up to 80% of our communication is non-verbal. So in addition to listening to what is being said, you must try to observe and interpret your spouse's tone, body language and facial expressions. The best way to do this is to try to maintain eye contact throughout the discussion. The more observant you become, the better you will be at interpreting your spouse's non-verbal cues.

For example, say you notice your spouse crossing their arms during a conversation; it might indicate that they are feeling very defensive or closed off. If they are frowning; it may mean that they do not agree with your version of events. Once you understand what these non-verbal cues mean, you can quickly decide what to do next.

#3. Express Empathy and Understanding

Effective communication requires that you exercise a lot of empathy. This is done best by trying to put yourself in your spouse's shoes. It's almost impossible to understand another person well enough if you have not walked in their shoes. Even if I don't understand their take on an issue, but I empathise with them, I validate their feelings.

For example, if your spouse is upset about something that happened at work, try to acknowledge their feelings by saying, "That must have been really frustrating for you." or, "I can see why this is upsetting you." When you empathise, you are showing that you care, and your spouse feels loved.

#4. Communicate Clearly and Honestly

Good communication happens when you endeavour to express your thoughts and feelings transparently. If you want to say something important to your spouse, try to go straight to the point. Don't muddle your communication by beating about the bush or discussing irrelevant things.

Also, use "I" statements instead of "You" statements, to avoid sounding accusatory. For example, instead of saying, "You never help me with the chores," say, "I feel overwhelmed when I have to do all the chores by myself." Your spouse is less likely to argue with you if you are only stating the facts from your position.

#5. Avoid Assumptions and Guesses

Don't presume to know what your spouse is thinking or feeling during a conversation. Instead, learn to ask clarifying questions. For example, if your spouse is very quiet during a discussion, don't assume they are angry or bitter with you. They may just be thinking or concentrating deeply. Go ahead and ask! Say something like, "Did something I said bother you?" or "Do you want me to give you a few minutes to process what I just said?" Since you are not a mind-reader, it's always much better to ask clarifying questions than to assume.

#6. Choose the Right Timing and Setting

Another skill that aids fruitful communication is learning to choose the right time and place for your important conversations. Avoid discussing serious issues when either of you is tired, hungry or distracted. We know, for instance, that low blood sugar levels can impair communication by causing confusion or irritability. It can also cause poor concentration.

These symptoms can hinder your ability to think clearly, process information properly, or articulate your thoughts effectively. Bringing up marital problems and challenges at the wrong time often leads to misunderstandings which of course defeat the aims of good communication.

#7. Be Open to Feedback

Being open to feedback while communicating or resolving conflict is crucial. It promotes mutual growth and helps you identify blind spots in your relationship. Constructive feedback can also provide new perspectives—and improve decision-making as long as you're both open to it. It ensures that your discussion remains productive and leads to positive outcomes.

Learn to accept your spouse's feedback without becoming defensive—

knowing that it's an opportunity for growth and improvement. For example, if your spouse mentions that you've been distant, instead of becoming defensive, respond with, "I didn't realize I was coming off that way. But I'm happy to talk about how I can be more present for you from now on."

#8. Resolve Conflicts Constructively

Every couple will have disagreements from time to time, but there are ways to handle your disagreements so that your relationship is strengthened and not weakened. One way is to focus on the issue at hand rather than attacking your spouse's character.

So, instead of saying, "You're so irresponsible," say, "I was upset when you forgot to pick up the groceries because it messed up our dinner plans." Saying that your spouse is irresponsible is attacking their character—which is likely to trigger a very defensive response. Saying "I was upset" on the other hand, is sharing your feelings without attacking your spouse.

#9. Express Gratitude and Appreciation

We all love to be appreciated and affirmed by the people who know and love us the best. That's why you have to get good at regularly acknowledging and valuing your spouse and their contribution to the progress of your relationship.

William Arthur Ward was quoted to have said, "**Feeling gratitude and not expressing it is like wrapping a present and not giving it.**"

Decide to make a habit of expressing gratitude daily. Send a quick text during the day to say, "I appreciate you taking care of the kids this morning." Better still, verbally express your gratitude to your spouse for something they have done—over dinner.

These are a few strategies for effective communication. Write out and ruminate on them so that you can implement some of them in your daily interactions. Also, take time regularly to reflect on which of these strategies are helping to deepen your marriage.

"The most important thing in communication is hearing what isn't said" – Peter Drucker

COUPLES DISCUSSION POINTS

- Which of the <u>nine</u> Communication strategies jumped out at you as potentially very helpful in your relationship?

  _____

  _____

  _____

  _____

- Which one of you is willing to take the lead in ensuring that you consistently apply what you are learning about Communication—in your relationship?

  _____

Your Premarital Journal

What thoughts, ideas, decisions and prayer points would you like to keep a record of after reading this part of the manual? Write them in the space below:

PRINCIPLE #5

EMBRACE YOUR ROLES AND RESPONSIBILITIES

"However, let each one of you love his wife as himself, and let the wife see that she respects her husband."
(Ephesians 5:33.) ESV.

A partnership is a cooperative relationship between two or more people who agree to share responsibility, liability and profit for a specific venture or goal. In your case, that venture is marriage. You both have dreams, goals and desires that you want to see accomplished. The only way you get to see those desires achieved is if you are both willing to do whatever it takes to get them done. That's where roles and responsibilities come in.

If you want healthy home-cooked food or a clean home, someone needs to make that happen. If you want to live comfortably, go away on romantic or family holidays, or raise creative and intelligent children, someone has to make it happen too. If you want your kids to learn a musical instrument or play football, someone must take them for practice. The point is that nothing great happens by itself.

So, it's important to negotiate and agree on who would be responsible for the different elements of what you wish to achieve as a couple. I'm not just talking about dividing up chores. Rather, I'm talking about creating shared understanding, respect, and teamwork that contributes to the overall well-being of the marriage. Without this process, the dynamics of your relationship can quickly spiral into resentment, frustration, and chaos. What I am saying is that roles and responsibilities should be agreed on—not assumed.

Here is why recognising roles and responsibilities matter:

1.) It Maintains Balance and Harmony in the Home.

If you and your partner have an agreed set of roles and responsibilities, it will help you to maintain balance and harmony in the home. When you mutually agree on your respective roles—whether it's managing finances, taking care of children, cleaning, or maintaining the household—there's less room for confusion or unmet expectations. This doesn't mean each partner has to conform to traditional gender roles, but instead, you should define roles based on your strengths, preferences, and availability. This creates a sense of teamwork that strengthens the bond between you and fosters a positive atmosphere in the home.

2.) It Promotes Strong Teamwork and Partnership.

Relationships thrive when you both work as a team. Clearly defined roles and responsibilities create a sense of partnership—where each one of you knows exactly what to expect from the other. Teamwork helps you feel equally involved in the relationship and reduces the chance of one person feeling overworked or overburdened.

3.) It Prevents Resentment from Developing.

One of the major risks of failing to define and embrace roles is the build-up of resentment. Often, one partner feels they are carrying a lot more than is fair. This soon leads to anger, frustration, and resentment. The overburdened person feels isolated—and starts to question their partner's commitment to the relationship altogether. This emotional toll can significantly damage the relationship and make it difficult to work through other challenges in the future.

4.) It Encourages Clear Communication.

Couples who embrace their roles and responsibilities also tend to communicate better naturally. You check in on each other, give feedback, and express gratitude. When challenges come, you are more open to review or change your roles because their is openness and mutual understanding.

5.) It Helps the Home Run More Efficiently.

Your house will run much more efficiently when roles are defined. It's like running a business; when everyone knows what they're supposed to do, tasks get done more smoothly and with less stress. Whether it's changing burnt light bulbs, paying bills on time, or making sure the house is cleaned regularly, understanding who is responsible for what, makes managing the home more efficient. Without a rigorous structure like this, important things fall through the cracks—leading to preventable tension and arguments.

6.) It Enchances Your Emotional and Mental Health.

Embracing your roles and responsibilities has significant benefits for your emotional and mental health. When you both feel like you are contributing fairly to the smooth running of the home and that your efforts are recognised and appreciated, you'll generally feel a sense of accomplishment. This, in turn, will create mutual respect and a supportive environment. On the other hand, when roles are not embraced, it can lead to burnout, especially for the person who is carrying the lion's share of the work. Over time, the strain can lead to anxiety, depression, or bitterness.

7.) It Sets a Positive Example For Your Children.

One day, God willing, you will have children. Embracing your roles and responsibilities will set a positive example for them. It will teach them about cooperation, teamwork, and the importance of taking their responsibilities seriously. Children who grow up in households where roles are clearly defined and respected—often learn to value contribution and teamwork. They are also more likely to carry those lessons into their adult relationships. Remember that children are constantly observing and learning from their parents, and the way roles and responsibilities are handled at home will shape their own expectations and behaviour later on in life.

What Happens When Roles Are Not Embraced?

If you don't take this issue seriously, several issues can arise:

1. **Unmet Expectations.**
2. **Feelings of Resentment.**
3. **Burnout and Poor Health.**
4. **Increased Conflict and Tension.**
5. **Diminished Respect and Trust.**
6. **A Poorly Run Home.**

7. **Loss of Intimacy.**

Conclusion:

The importance of recognising and embracing responsibilities and roles in your marriage relationship cannot be overstated. It creates a platform for a healthy, respectful, and balanced relationship. When you take the time to discuss and agree upon your roles and responsibilities, it should lead to reduced stress, smoother communication, and a supportive partnership. The home is more likely to be a place of harmony—rather than tension. But if you neglect this important issue, it can result in unnecessary conflict, resentment, and even the breakdown of the relationship.

COUPLES DISCUSSION POINTS

- Go through the list on the next <u>two</u> pages, and <u>tick</u> the roles you expect to be responsible for—and the roles you expect your spouse to take on.

- Start by doing the exercise separately for 5 minutes—then come together to compare and discuss your results.

_____

_____

PRACTICAL ROLES AND RESPONSIBILITIES

	ME	MY SPOUSE
Washing & staking dishes	☐	☐
Doing the laundry	☐	☐
Ironing & folding clothes	☐	☐
Cleaning the bathroom	☐	☐
Vacuuming the carpets	☐	☐
Making the beds	☐	☐
Managing & pay utility bills	☐	☐
Grocery shopping	☐	☐
Mopping the floors	☐	☐
Managing your insurances	☐	☐
Planning & cooking meals	☐	☐
Cleaning out the fridge	☐	☐
Loading & unloading the dishwasher	☐	☐
Wiping down kitchen countertops	☐	☐
Planning & searching for holidays	☐	☐
Scrubbing the bathtub / shower	☐	☐
Cleaning home appliances	☐	☐
Disinfecting & cleaning the toilet	☐	☐
Organising closets and drawers	☐	☐
Changing the bed linens	☐	☐
Taking out the trash	☐	☐
Sorting & recycling waste	☐	☐
Locking up at night (security)	☐	☐
Cleaning the windows	☐	☐

	ME	MY SPOUSE
Mending clothes, buttons	☐	☐
Driving the family around	☐	☐
Managing the family finances	☐	☐
The spiritual leader	☐	☐
Taking care of indoor plants, deco.	☐	☐
Buying gifts for family & friends	☐	☐
Disciplining the Children	☐	☐
Shopping for children	☐	☐
Sending out cards (e.g. Christmas)	☐	☐
Polishing silverware & furniture	☐	☐
Christmas & Easter decorations	☐	☐
Entertaining visitors / family	☐	☐
Caring for pets (e.g. fish, rabbit)	☐	☐
Raking or cleaning the yard	☐	☐
Maintaining security alarm	☐	☐
Mowing the lawn	☐	☐
Weeding the garden	☐	☐
Cleaning the garage or store	☐	☐
Unclogging toilets & drains	☐	☐
Checking smoke & fire detectors	☐	☐
Replacing light bulbs	☐	☐
Dusting and cleaning furniture	☐	☐
Maintaining household appliances	☐	☐
TOTALS:	☐	☐

Discussion Question:

—How well were your **desires** mirrored in your spouse's list?

Your Premarital Journal

What thoughts, ideas, decisions and prayer points would you like to keep a record of after reading this part of the manual? Write them in the space below:

PRINCIPLE #6

MANAGE YOUR MONEY BIBLICALLY

"For this reason, a man shall leave his father and mother and be joined to his wife, and the two shall become one flesh'; so then they are no longer two, but one flesh. Therefore what God has joined together, let not man separate." (Mark 10:7-9.)

There is a battle for your finances, similar to the fight raging for your soul. Satan knows that if he can mess up your finances, he can mess up other parts of your life too. We know that 7 out of every 10 couples who get a divorce, cite money issues as one of their top three reasons for the breakage.

Almost half of all our prisoners are in prison because of money scams and crimes. The drug epidemic and the indiscriminate waves of illegal activity across our society are both connected to greed and money problems. So, if you want to strengthen your marriage, you need to understand money and learn how to use it well.

As you no doubt know, your marriage is a partnership. And you know that no partnership can work well if there is no agreement. The Prophet Amos made this very clear when he said, **"Can two walk together unless they agree to do so?"** (Amos 3:3.)

The answer is obvious. You can't get on as a couple without agreeing on where you are going and why you should go on that journey together. This is so important, especially in the area of finances. So, I'd like to suggest **5** crucial ways to avoid this problem in your marriage.

1.) Make sure you have similar perspectives on the issue of money.

Here is a list of money perspectives and principles that you can both discuss and adopt:

"God is our Master and Controller, not money."

"All the money we have actually belongs to God, and we are just stewards of it."

"We are committed to avoiding debt and extravagant living at all costs."

"We agree that any money we have belongs to both of us, not one of us."

"We endeavour to save a portion of every pound that comes in."

"We are committed to proportional giving."

"We will be faithful caretakers of the money God has given us to manage."

Having similar (Bible-backed) perspectives on money will strengthen your relationship and reduce most of the money problems couples have.

2.) Make a habit of praying together about your finances.

Don't make major financial decisions without praying together about it.

This makes sure that you invite God's wisdom and guidance into your financial affairs. Couples that pray together, stay together. Why? Because prayer will connect you to the help and power of God like nothing else will. So make praying together about your finances a priority.

3.) Endeavour to talk openly and honestly about how best to manage your money.

If you are struggling in some aspect of your money management, talk it over and find uplifting ways to help each other. Men are generally more reserved when it comes to opening up about their money problems. This is because we tend to equate our effectiveness with the amount of money we make or have. If you are a Christian man, your identity and value come from the God who made you, not from the money you make.

4.) Plan a joint budget that will hopefully get you to your desired place financially.

It's one thing to set a goal to be financially responsible or free. It's another thing to develop a plan and do the hard work it takes. Creating a budget is where you'll need to start the process. Sit down and work out a budget that respects both of your views, needs, contributions, and financial goals. For instance: How much do you both have coming in? How much should you spend and still have enough left each month to save and give? What can you reduce to have more money left over at the end of the month? If you both carefully answer these questions and design a complimentary budget to achieve your goals, you'll have conquered one of the most divisive challenges in marriage.

5.) Humbly seek guidance from people who have a track record of managing their money well.

When facing financial challenges or decisions, don't hesitate to seek advice from trusted Christian advisers, counsellors, or expert financial mentors. Why? Because the Bible teaches us to do so. Solomon wrote, **"Get all the advice you can, and you will succeed; without it you will fail."** (Proverbs 15:22.) GNB.

Never let pride prevent you from pursuing wisdom and knowledge from people who have achieved what you both wish to achieve. Truth be told, people who are successful in any area of their life, are often very eager to share how they succeeded. All you need to do is humbly ask!

"Where there is no counsel, the people fall; But in the multitude of counselors there is safety." (Proverbs 11:14.)

NINE FINANCIAL VALUES ALL SUCCESSFUL CHRISTIAN COUPLES HAVE

1.) They Respect Money.

2.) They Spend Less Than They Earn.

3.) They Plug the Leaks in Their Financial Tub.

4.) They Honour Their Heavenly Father.

5.) They Pay Themselves a Portion of All They Earn.

6.) They Save a Portion of All They Earn.

7.) They Invest a Portion of All They Earn.

8.) They Choose Profitable Financial Vehicles.

9.) They Insure Against Possible Setbacks.

> For a more detailed account of these <u>nine</u> values or principles, and how to build lasting wealth for your family, check out my book titled… **'Surplus Money — How to get out of debt, build lasting wealth and leave a legacy of abundance.'** on all good online retailers.

Here is a Summary of these Nine Wise Money Values:

1.) Respect Money, but don't love it.

I've noticed that people weighed down by debt usually don't have a healthy respect for money either. So, money (like a disrespected lover) simply leaves them for someone else. Whatever you respect, you attract—and whatever you dishonour, you repel. If you don't take care of the pennies, you are never going to have enough pounds.

When I talk about respecting money, I'm not talking about loving it. The love of money is wrong because it elevates money above God. That's why the Bible warns us about loving money. It says:

> **"For the love of money is a root of all kinds of evil, for which some have strayed from the faith in their greediness, and pierced themselves through with many sorrows."** (1 Timothy 6:10.)

When you respect money, you don't waste it, abuse it or gamble it away. You don't use it to purchase things to impress people who can't be bothered about you. Instead, when you respect money, you take good care of it. You appreciate its value and you endeavour to maximise every penny. You do that because you understand that it ultimately belongs to God.

So, you keep good track of where your money is going. You act as a responsible trustee. You manage it wisely, and you protect it from thieves, unexpected disasters, and get-rich-quick schemes. When you go out of your way to respect money in this way, God will bless your faithfulness. That's precisely what Jesus taught and promised us in Luke 16:10-12. He said:

> **"Whoever can be trusted with very little can also be trusted with much, and whoever is dishonest with very little will also be dishonest with much. So if you have not been trustworthy in handling worldly wealth, who will trust you with true riches? And if you have not been trustworthy with someone else's property, who will give you property of your own?"**

My point is that the way you handle the little money God initially gives you will determine the amount God can eventually trust you with. So, if you are wondering why you are where you are financially, check how you've been stewarding the money you have.

2.) Spend Less Than You Earn.

Telling you to spend less than you earn seems so unnecessary. You already know this. But, as you know, common sense is not always common. One of the reasons so many of us spend more than we earn is because we've embraced the ungodly culture of the world we live in.

Only a few decades ago, my parent's generation had to save for months to pay for their suits, their furniture or their vehicles. Why? Because although loans were available back then, Banks only gave them out to people who wanted to purchase **assets**—like houses, businesses, or products to sell.

People never used to go to their bank managers to ask for money to buy consumables—like food, clothes, designer shoes or handbags. Sadly, that's exactly what the **credit system** has done to us today. It allows you to 'take a loan' to buy anything your heart desires. That's the reason most people spend more than they earn.

The credit system has awakened in us a spirit of **greed**—and our carnal nature has latched onto it. We have all become more covetous and materialistic. Nevertheless, we can be free from the allurement of easy credit.

Here are three suggestions:

a.) Get rid of your Credit Cards.

There is nothing your Credit Card can do that your Debit Cards cannot do; apart from getting you into debt. So get rid of those Credit and Store Cards, until you have paid off all your debts, and learnt to spend less than you earn.

b.) Live on a strict temporary Budget.

If you are in debt, get onto a strict temporary budget. I'm calling it strict because it is going to hurt for a while. But after your debt is cleared, you will be glad you did it. You are going to survive for as long as it takes on the barest minimum. No expensive phone tariffs; no expensive TV networks; no pedicures, manicures, or gym membership; and no coffees and doughnuts at Starbucks—until your debt is cleared or minimised.

c.) Find creative ways to reduce your spending.

There are hundreds of innovative ways to reduce your spending or stop your money from being wasted. I will cover some of these ways in the next point.

3.) Plug the Leaks to Your Financial Tub.

Money is like water in a bathtub. If more water is flowing out than flowing in, your tub will never fill up. So if you want to take a bath, you need to stop the leaks. You need to make sure the water stays in the tub. It's the same with your money. You need to find where your money is going and stop the leaks. That way, you can save more and have enough when you need it.

Here are several areas you could be leaking money:

- Paying more than necessary for services.

- Living in a ridiculously expensive area.
- Paying more tax than you are required to.
- Paying high interest rates on loans and credit facilities.
- Eating out or buying ready-made food regularly.
- Driving a car that you can't afford yet.
- Paying for services you don't maximise or use.
- Leaving lights on all day and all night.
- Driving uneconomical or fuel-guzzling vehicles.
- Living in a poorly heat-insulated property.
- Paying penalties and late fees for being careless.
- Buying more than you need and throwing out the rest.
- Living in a property that's out of your league.
- Spending more than you can afford on your extended family.

If you sit down and look at where your money is going, you can find several "leaks" and stop them right away. But finding and stopping the leaks is just the beginning. The next important step is to use the money you save to pay off your debt or loans consistently. Taking action is what always makes the difference.

If you don't do this, you are wasting the resources you have, whether you realize it or not. Don't expect any financial miracles if you keep wasting what you already have. Sometimes, when I hear people praying for financial help, I think their requests are unlikely to be answered. Why? Because they keep wasting what they've already been given. God doesn't promise to bless us so we can keep wasting His resources.

Jesus gave us a parable to that effect in Luke, chapter 16. It says:

> **"There was a certain rich man who had a steward, and an accusation was brought to him that this man was wasting his goods. So he called him and said to him, "What is this I hear about you? Give an account of your stewardship, for you can no longer be steward."**

The purpose of this parable was to teach us that the **rich man** (which is a metaphor for God) doesn't want his stewards (which is a metaphor for you and I) to be wasteful. The steward in this parable lost his job and the favour of his boss because he wasted his master's goods. If, unlike the steward, you diligently take care of the obvious money holes in your life, God will graciously and lavishly open the windows of heaven over your life—because you have shown Him that you are diligent and not wasteful.

4.) Honour your Heavenly Father.

Many people think that the sole purpose of money is to spend it on themselves. If you see money in that way, you are making a huge mistake. One reason God blesses you with money is because He requires a portion of it. Yes, you heard that right! God needs you to release a portion of the money He has blessed you with, to build His Kingdom on earth.

"Why does God need my money?", I hear you ask.

Firstly, the money you call yours is not yours at all.

The Bible says: **"The earth is the Lord's and everything in it..."** (Psalms 24:1.)

That means, everything you have technically, belongs to God. And as a member of His family, He wants you to contribute a portion of what He has given you to His Family on earth—called the Church. What a privilege it is to be called upon by God to give something back to the Church that has fed and helped you spiritually and emotionally all these years.

Secondly, God saved you and left you here to build His Kingdom.

God's part was to save, heal, and deliver you from death and Satan. Your part is to take care of His Church and His Ministers on this side of eternity. If you understand this divine principle, you'll never again struggle to release a portion of your income to God. Your heavenly Father has commanded every one of His Children to put a portion of their income aside for His use. The Bible calls this portion of your income, the tithe or the first fruit.

As you willingly and generously release that portion of your income to God, you'll be putting God's Kingdom agenda first. And the good news is that He promises to reward you bountifully. Just make up your mind to honour and obey God in this holy ordinance of giving a portion of your income to God through His Church.

Here is what the Bible says about giving to God:

> "But this I say: He who sows sparingly will also reap sparingly, and he who sows bountifully will also reap bountifully." (2 Corinthians 9:6.)

> "Honour the LORD with your possessions, and with the first-fruits of all your increase; so your barns will be filled with plenty, and your vats will overflow with new wine." (Proverbs 3:9-10.)

> "Bring all the tithes into the storehouse, that there may be food in My house, and try Me now in this," says the LORD of hosts, "If I will not open for you the windows of heaven and pour out for you such blessing that there will not be room enough to receive it. And I will rebuke the devourer for your sakes, so that he will not destroy the fruit of your ground, nor shall the vine fail to bear fruit for you in the field," says the LORD of hosts" (Malachi 3:10-11.)

> "And let us not grow weary while doing good, for in due season we shall reap if we do not lose heart. Therefore, as we have opportunity, let us do good to all, especially to those who are of the household of faith." (Galatians 6:9-10.).

Your Heavenly Father wants you to set apart the first portion of your income or gain for Kingdom use. That's what the Scriptures clearly teach us. If you will carefully obey God's will, the rest of your income will be blessed; because when the first part of your money is blessed, the rest is blessed too.

I know that you may be tempted to think that preachers only say things like this because they want your money, but nothing can be further from the truth. God-fearing Ministers teach this principle, because that's what the Bible tells them to teach, and because they don't want you to miss out on God's promise to bless you for obeying His Word.

> "Give, and it will be given to you: good measure, pressed down, shaken together, and running over will be put into your bosom. For with the same measure that you use, it will be measured back to you." (Luke 6:38.)

So, make sure that you honour the wishes of your heavenly Father. You won't regret it!

5.) Pay Yourself a Portion of All You Earn.

I can't remember where I first heard this financial advice, but it's helped me a lot over the years. At the beginning of my working life, I spent almost every penny of my income on things I wanted right away. I'm sure that I did that because I had a scarcity mindset.

The banks instituted profitable savings accounts and ISAs to encourage savings, but I didn't think I could afford it. Then one day, as I was getting ready to travel abroad, it hit me, that if I had an accident and died on that trip, my wife and two young children would struggle financially. I was in my early thirties with no life insurance, no investments, no pension, and very little savings.

It was around that time that I first heard the phrase: **Pay yourself first.** A motivational speaker explained that we work hard to make money for others, but we seldom think of ourselves. Then he painted a vivid picture of what paying ourselves first could look like in ten, twenty, or thirty years.

If you don't want to be a slave to everyone—including your mortgage company, car loan company, electric company, gas company, and phone company—you must learn to pay yourself first. You can't afford to wake up every morning and hand everything you earn to these companies. Unfortunately, many people do.

The idea is to make sure that you put something away for your future before you spend a penny on every other thing that begs for your money. God comes first for me, so I pay my tithes and offerings first, and then I pay myself next.

Here is what I chose to do:

1.) **I decided to pay myself a minimum of 10% of my income every month.**

2.) **I decided to put that money into a savings account, and not touch it until I found a long-term investment to put it into.**

I can't tell you how satisfying it was to see the money I paid myself grow for the very first time in my life. It changed everything for me. It wasn't just some savings I planned to use up on my next vacation. It was money I put towards my future. It became a big part of my pension. And, it became proof that I valued myself enough to invest some of my earnings into my destiny.

Here are **four** reasons to pay yourself first, (or second, if you are a child of God):

1.) **The future will come whether you like it or not, and the only thing you'll have is what you put away for it.**

2.) **Paying yourself first (or second) helps you to manage the rest of your money more wisely.**

3.) **When you see your money growing, you feel good about yourself and less insecure about your future.**

4.) **Paying yourself first (or second) can help you enjoy a more financially comfortable future.**

If I had only understood this concept when I was much younger, I wouldn't have wasted several years putting that money into savings accounts. I would have immediately put that money into a Pension Plan every month. Why?

Because that's exactly what a pension plan is designed to do well. Plus, in the UK at least, it is a very tax-efficient way to save. What I'm saying is that you would see your pension grow exponentially as a result of the discipline of paying yourself a portion of everything you earn.

Make Your Future a Priority

If you are like most reasonable people, you work really hard all year long. You pay your bills, you pay your taxes, and you pay for food, shelter and transportation. Great! But what do you pay yourself for working so hard? For many people, the answer is Nothing! Why? Because they never made themselves a priority. So this is what often happens.

They turn 50, 55 or 60 years old and have a little health challenge or get made redundant for a few months. They soon fall behind on their mortgage, and the bank threatens to repossess their home. They planned to retire at 65—but they can't afford to do so any more because they still have debts to pay off. That's what happens if you don't pay yourself a portion of what you earn regularly.

The goose that lays the golden egg dies penniless, so to speak! You've worked like a dog, but when it's time to reap the harvest of your effort, the fridge is empty and the financial institutions ask you to turn in your credit card. That's what happens to a lot of people, but it doesn't need to happen to you and your spouse—if you decide to pay yourself a portion of everything you earn.

6.) Save a Portion of All You Earn.

It is foolish to spend every penny you earn. That's why people have huge debts or stay poor. But you don't have to be in that number if you understand and embrace the principles I am sharing with you in this book. The majority of wealthy people are not wealthy because they are lucky or because they were born into wealth. They are rich because they practice 'rich' financial habits.

One of those wealthy financial habits is to save a portion of everything you earn. They do it for three main reasons.

  1.) They do it to build capital.

  2.) They do it to take advantage of deals and opportunities, or

  3.) They do it to build a 'rainy day' fund.

Building Capital.

Wealthy people know that they can borrow money cheaply from financial institutions to acquire appreciable assets. However, very few financial institutions will loan you 100% of the cost of your asset. They want you to have a bit of skin in the game too. Consequently, they will only loan you between 60% and 80% of the amount needed.

Wealthy people know this, so they learn to put money away to have the deposit they need to purchase the assets they want. When you have capital, access to more capital becomes easier. Access to deals open up; and financial institutions will be more than happy to invest their money into your asset accumulation.

Take Advantage of Great Deals.

I remember getting a phone call from a friend during the financial downturn in 2009. He told me that Banks in America, were trying to offload hundreds of foreclosed houses. The previous owners lost their jobs and couldn't afford to pay their mortgages. Three and four-bedroom houses were being auctioned off for $10,000 to $15,000 during the crisis.

My wife and I were able to buy a couple of those houses outright with money from our savings. How was that possible? It was possible because we had developed the habit of saving a portion of our income every month over the previous 8 or 9 years. We had the capital to take advantage of great deals when they popped up—and we didn't have to borrow a penny to do so.

Aim to save at least 10% of your income every month. But even if you can't afford the whole 10% when you start out, do at least 5%. I promise you, it will give you the capital or deposit you need for assets or great deals when they show up. Saving regularly prepares you to take advantage of great opportunities.

Create A Rainy Day Fund

Saving a portion of your income regularly will also give you a 'rainy day' pot of money. People tend to forget that nothing lasts forever. You may buy the best quality refrigerator on the market, but it will stop working one day. And when it does, you shouldn't have to buy another one on credit.

Your car will need changing, your settee will wear out, your cooker will pack up, and your bed or mattress will need to be replaced. When they do, you will be able to walk into a shop and pay cash for a new one if you learn to save a portion of everything you earn.

Why is this important? It's important because everything costs more on credit. For a start, the credit card companies understand the psychology of spending. They know that we would happily pay more for an item when we purchase it with credit.

Some years ago, my wife bought a leather bag from a seller in Spain. The vendor told her he was willing to sell it to her for €120. My wife, not willing to pay the full price for anything, told him that his pricing was unreasonable. Finally, he came down to about €60, and he was ready to take any credit card.

My wife simply brought €30 cash out of her purse and told him that that was all she could pay. Guess what, he sold her the bag for €30. The reason I'm telling you this story is because this seller would never have accepted €30 if my wife had brought out her credit card to pay for it.

Better Credit Rating.

Saving regularly can potentially improve your credit rating with your bank as well. Customers who maintain consistent saving habits are usually rated higher than customers who don't. Your bank will see you as advantageous to their bottom line; since they typically use your savings as loans to other customers while it's sitting in your account. So, learn to save.

Peace of Mind.

Another benefit of saving a portion of every Pound, Dollar, Euro, or any currency you earn, is peace of mind. You worry less! You stress less!! And, you are less anxious!!! Why? Because you don't have to wonder how to pay for all your regular and unexpected bills. You have a little extra for a rainy day. You have 'margin'!

I remember when my wife and I paid off our last loan over three decades ago, we had an extra £200 a month to save. We was so happy to have that extra money, so we put it towards our mortgage. That extra money (plus some overtime jobs) helped us pay off our mortgage 11 years early. That's what 'margin' can do for you.

7.) Invest a Portion of All You earn.

When you start to see some margin in your income, it's time to start investing. It's time to look for creative ways of growing your extra money or rapidly reducing your liabilities. Saving money in a bank alone no longer produces real wealth like it used to do in the past—unless you have 30 to 40 years to leave it there.

Saving money in a bank used to be a great way to invest in the 80's and 90's when interest rates were in double digits, and compound interest did wonders for your money. Nowadays, the interest the banks pay hardly keeps up with inflation. And if you manage to get a fair rate paid to you, it will usually be taxed to death.

I am not certified to teach on the intricacies of investment, so I will not attempt to do that in this book. Nevertheless, there are tonnes of excellent investment books and training courses that can do a much better job than I can ever do. If you need that level of knowledge, please go to the experts. My goal here is to show you the importance of investing—if you want to grow wealth for your future and your family.

I teach people to build wealth through (what I call) an **investment vehicle**. An investment vehicle is a specific tool of investing that allows you to build wealth and increase your net worth over time. Here are some examples of investment vehicles you can use to build wealth and increase your net worth.

Stocks and Shares:

You buy stocks or shares in other people's businesses and share in the profits they generate.

Providing a Service:

You employ people to provide a service that pays you more than you need to pay your employees, and you pocket the difference.

Manufacturing:

You pay people to make or produce products that you can sell for a profit online or in a shop.

Established or startup companies:

You invest in a startup company and own a percentage of the business.

Angel Investor:

You loan capital to a business person for a cut of the profit he or she makes.

Speculating:

You hunt for and buy assets that appreciate in value (like a vintage car or a high-value wristwatch). Or you can invest in a service that produces a regular income (like a Property or an Uber Driver).

Front-loading your Pension Funds:

You put as much money into your pension plan as you are allowed by law as early as possible—since pensions are the most tax-efficient forms of investments today. Then, you leave it to grow until it can provide you with a healthy income. In the United Kingdom, you can start to draw on that income from the age of 55.

You will, of course, need to do your own research into what might work best for you. There are no silver bullets, but with a little bit of knowledge and wisdom, you can usually find two or more streams of income that would work well for you—if you are patient.

My Preference.

I personally prefer to invest in the following four investment pots.

Brick and Mortar Investment:

For instance, my wife and I bought our first home in 1987. Then it was worth around £46,000. When our family got larger and we had to move, we decided to keep that flat as an investment property and rent it out. That property is now worth about £300,000 and has provided continuous rental income for us for more than 30 years. I'm convinced that good old 'brick and mortar' is still one of the best investments around—if you learn how to manage it well.

National Savings and Investment Bonds:

I like this form of investment because my capital is guaranteed by the British Government and I get a percentage of the stakes awarded almost every month. In a good year, some investors can get up to 10 times more return on investment, than if they had put their money in a Savings Account.

My Occupational Pension:

I invest good chunks of money—over and above the recommended percentage of my salary—into my pension fund because the Government gives tax relief on the money paid into the pension pot. My employer contributes an additional amount to the pot every month and the UK Government relieves me of paying tax on all my contributions. It's no wonder that I love the British Pension system!

Shares in Banks and other profitable companies that pay dividends:

The companies I love to invest in are companies that pay dividends annually or bi-annually. I particularly like this option because, in addition to the dividends I get paid once or twice a year, the share prices generally keep rising year on year, over the long term. I haven't sold any of my shares yet, but when I do decide to sell them, some of them may be worth six or seven times what they costed when we first got them many years ago.

Every one of these investment streams (and more) are available to you. So start wherever you can, and build from there. Remember that investments are long-term commitments that require patience —and patience never fails to deliver. Also, remember that the sooner you start, the quicker you will start to see results.

8.) Choose Your Financial Vehicles.

A Financial Vehicle is any financial tool or instrument that helps you make money not only when you are working, but more importantly, when you are sleeping. An example of one of my Financial Vehicles is my **writing**. I research and write books to help people with specific challenges and problems they have in the areas of Marriage, Faith, Family, and Finances.

I put in the work at the start of the process, and can usually recuperate any money I spend getting the book to market within the first year of releasing it. However, what really excites me is the fact that I can keep earning money on the books I write, 10 or 20 years after first publishing them.

I call writing and publishing my Financial Vehicle because it is taking me towards my financial goals, even when I'm sleeping.

Here are a few other examples of possible Financial Vehicles:

- Song Writing
- Making Music
- Selling Information Videos
- Selling Training Videos
- Investing in Property
- Buying & Selling goods online
- Providing a useful Service for People
- Advertising Products for Manufacturers
- Importing and Exporting profitable products
- Trading Forex, Shares, Stocks, Indices and even Cryptos.

I am convinced that each person has (or can discover) one or more gifts or abilities, that can be developed enough to become financially profitable. The question is, what can you do or learn to do, that can take you closer to your financial destination?

Some years ago, after teaching a group of people on money matters, I challenged the group to go back and think about what they could do to make extra money each month. What amazed me at the time, was what they all came up with within a month.

Some made custom jewellery, some baked artful cakes, and some cooked and packaged special African delicacies. Others got into photography, videography, and drawing or portrait painting. One person brushed up on her hair styling skills and now owns a hair boutique. That was over 17 years ago, and some of those people are now making a living from their crafts.

We serve a creative God. One look at the Universe makes that very clear. But He didn't stop there, He made you in His image and likeness. That means you have the ability or potential to be creative as well. I want to challenge you and your spouse to sit down together to discuss ways of capitalising on your God-given creativity.

Income Streams

Before you choose the right financial vehicle or vehicles to take you to your desired financial destination, it's important to know and understand the seven income streams by which people make money. Here is a list:

1.) Earned Income

2.) Interest Income

3.) Profit Income

4.) Dividend Income

5.) Rental Income

6.) Capital Gains Income

7.) Royalty Income

Let's take a look at them one by one:

Earned Income.

Earned income is money earned from time spent working for someone. A good example is the salary you get paid at a job. Here you trade your time for money. Since your time is limited and you only get paid once for every week or month of working, this kind of income is very limited.

Profit Income.

Profit income is money earned for selling things for more than it cost to buy or to make. Let's say you buy a rundown classic old vehicle from an auctioneer for £2000. You get it fixed and rejuvenated for another £500. You then sell it to a car enthusiast for £3500. The profit of £1000 you make from that transaction is profit income.

Interest Income.

Interest Income is money earned from loans you make to people or money deposited into financial institutions. Typically, when you deposit money into a savings account or to fund a project, the organisation will pay you back your capital with an agreed interest. That interest payment is your interest income.

Dividend Income.

Dividend Income is another form of income that can yield great dividends. It is usually better than interest income because you are not only paid a share of the success of the company as a shareholder, but the original shares you bought, could be worth 40%, 80%, or even 150% more when you decide to sell them. The money they pay you annually or bi-annually is your dividend, but the amount you get for selling your shares for more than you bought them is called Capital Gains.

Rental Income.

Rental Income is money you make from buying and renting out assets like property or land. Although the value and rent of the property can fluctuate, they generally move upwards with time, if your property is in a safe and desirable area. The real money can often be made when you decide to sell your asset. Again, the gain you make from selling an asset for more than you bought it is called Capital Gains.

Capital Gains Income.

As already mentioned above, money made from selling an asset (like a house or a piece of land), over and above what you paid for it is called Capital Gains Income. Although this could be a great source of income, most countries have tax laws that eat into your profit. However, with the help of tax experts and thoughtful planning, there are usually ways to minimise these annoying tax penalties.

Royalty Income.

Royalty income is money you make from ideas, processes and products you sell or licence for others to use. Examples would be the music you compose or make; books you write; inventions you create; patents you register; or products you license. This is probably the best income source, because you work once on your idea or product, and they can keep producing continuous income for you for years to come. The only challenge, of course, is to create something unique that people want for years and years to come. But with thoughtful planning, hard work, and inspiration, it can be done.

How to Find Your Profitable Financial Vehicle.

Here is a list of what to do to discover and deploy a profitable financial vehicle:

1. Do an inventory of all your natural gifts, talents, and abilities.

2. Research all the profitable ventures, products and services available to you today.

3. Make a list of all the things you can see yourself doing, creating or servicing.

4. Choose one venture you can start to grow in your spare time.

5. Spend a few months getting some training in your chosen field.

6. Get to work on your chosen niche.

> For a more detailed breakdown of the six steps above, and how to build lasting wealth for your family, check out my book titled **'Surplus Money — How to get out of debt, build lasting wealth, and leave a legacy of abundance.'** on all good online retailers.

9.) Insure Against Setbacks.

We have seen that making money and striving hard to keep it, is one half of the challenge. The other half is to protect the wealth you have made—for your future and for your family. The way you do that is by keeping everything you have, properly and comprehensively insured.

Insurance is an awesome idea because it allows you to protect your assets and your life for as little as £25 a month—depending on your age or the value of what you want to insure, of course. In my opinion, that's a small price to pay to protect the fruit of your labour and to give you peace of mind.

Nobody ever expects their home to burn down, but if it does and you are not insured, you could lose everything. On the other hand, if you are insured, you can rest assured that your Insurance Company will accommodate you in the short term, and even build you back your home in the months to come. Therefore, insuring your assets should be a no-brainer.

Here are 5 important areas of insurance to consider:

- Life Insurance
- Health Insurance
- Home Insurance
- Travel Insurance
- A Will—which is not technically an insurance product, but ensures that your money and assets go where you want them to go—if anything should happen to you.

Life Insurance:

If you are married you need a Life Insurance policy to protect your spouse and your children. If you get Life Insurance while you are still young, it would be extremely cheap. Why? Because the insurance companies see younger people as low-risk clients.

The exact amount you need will depend on your circumstances. But as a rule of thumb, I often suggest an amount that will cover all your liabilities (including your mortgage), plus a year's worth of extra money to keep your family protected if you are not around.

As of today, a healthy 32-year-old male can get a Life Insurance Cover of up to £300,000 for less than £35 a month. Now, why would you not be willing to spend £35 a month to protect and provide for the most precious people in your life? If you are willing to spend £45 a month for your mobile phone, or £40 a month for your Satellite TV subscription; £35 a month for peace of mind should be a no-brainer.

Accident Insurance:

Accident insurance is another form of supplementary protection you should consider, especially if your career or job puts you at risk of accidents or injury. This type of insurance provides an additional layer of financial protection if you become injured.

It is often designed to cover all or part of your medical examination, treatment, hospital stays, physical or mental therapies, or the cost of drugs. Many of these policies may also pay out a fixed amount of money to help cover lost wages if you are unable to work for several weeks or months.

Health Insurance:

In the UK, where I live, we are blessed with a second-to-none, almost free, National Health Service. That means many of us don't bother with private health insurance. However, that can't be said for many other parts of the world. So this section is mainly for you if you live in a Country that either has a poor Health Service or a paid Health Service.

The Health Insurance is similar to the Accident Insurance in that it pays for medical, surgical and dental expenses. No one plans to get sick or hurt, but some of us will need medical care at some point in our lives —because we live in a broken world. The question is: If you do fall sick or need an operation that keeps you out of action for an extended time, can you survive financially?

Can you take care of your regular bills? Can you pay for hospitalisation, treatment, nurses, and the drugs needed? Can you keep your rent or mortgage paid up? If the answer is 'no', you may want to consider health insurance.

Even if you go through life untouched by any major sickness, you'll have constant peace of mind; and the satisfaction of knowing that your finances are protected at all times. As you get older, I can promise you that you'll come to value peace of mind, instead of stressing over money issues.

Home Insurance:

Home insurance protects your property and your belongings. There are three main types of home insurance: buildings insurance, contents insurance and combined buildings and contents insurance.

Buildings insurance covers the cost of repairing damage to the structure of your property. This includes the walls, windows and roof as well as permanent fixtures and fittings such as baths, toilets and fitted kitchens. As a general rule, your building insurance will also cover the cost of rebuilding your house from the ground up.

Contents insurance, on the other hand, covers the cost of replacing your belongings in your home—if they are damaged, destroyed or stolen. If you own your home, home insurance is obligatory, because if anything bad happens to your home, your insurance will cover the cost of it. If you are renting, you should at least have a content insurance policy to cover the theft of, or damage to your belongings. It is well worth it!

Travel Insurance:

Travel or holiday insurance is designed to give you extra protection if your holiday doesn't go as planned. It is particularly important to take out travel insurance if you are travelling independently because you may find yourself stranded with no way to get home and no one to help sort out your holiday problem.

Travel insurance can protect you against unexpected medical emergencies if you fall sick; delayed or cancelled flights; missed transport for reasons beyond your control; stolen, damaged or lost luggage, money or passport; and personal injury.

If you don't have travel insurance and any of these things happen, you may have to cover the cost out of your own pocket while you are away. And, from experience, I can tell you that it is never cheap.

Make a Will:

Another thing a lot of people neglect to do is to make out a will when they are strong and healthy. We may all hope to live for a hundred years, but the reality is that only a fraction of humanity will ever reach that age. The average life expectancy nowadays is closer to 70 years. Three out of every ten people will die before they reach 70. So the wise thing to do is to be clear on where we want our wealth to go when we are no longer here. A will is a legal document that expresses how you want your money, property or estate to be distributed when you die.

It is important to take a few minutes to write down your desires in this respect—knowing that you can always change it next year, or in five years—if your circumstances change. Don't procrastinate. Get yourself a Will-Kit from a High Street shop or the internet. Fill it out and sign it. It's as simple as that! Of course, you can eventually get your will professionally written when you have plenty of money and assets.

A Paradigm Shift is Needed

Many people feel that spending money on insurance or a pension is a waste of time and money, but it really isn't. You are simply protecting yourself against the uncertainties and unpredictabilities of life. It doesn't matter how spiritual or careful you are, if you live long enough, you will pass through the fires of life.

Why? Because you live in a broken world, and bad things happen. Disasters happen! Loss happens!! And accidents happen!!! So, instead of complaining about things you can't change, spend your energy trying to mitigate them.

The Bible says: **Many are the afflictions of the righteous...** (Psalms 34:19.) That's right! Even the righteous will have many afflictions. Good people will have many hardships, many ordeals, many challenges, and many setbacks. You don't have to do anything wrong to be hit by a misfortune or an illness. You just have to be alive! Fortunately, the second half of the verse says, "**...but the LORD delivers him out of them all.**"

Yes, God did promise to deliver the righteous out of all their troubles, but He didn't promise to pay for the damages caused. He didn't promise to pay the loss of your wages while you are sick. He didn't promise to pay redundancy or your pension. All He promised, is to deliver you from the situation and spare your life.

It's what you've **sown** that returns back to you—thirty, sixty or a hundredfold. It's what you've invested that pays you dividends. It's what you've prudently set aside for the rainy day, that would stop you from going hungry. So do your best to **insure** your property, your health, your career, and even your life. If you do, you won't regret it, and you will be leaving a good example for your children.

COUPLE'S DISCUSSION POINTS:

- What things stood out to you in this part of the manual?

  _____

  _____

  _____

- What decisions do you and your spouse need to make to manage your money well and never have to worry about your future?

  _____

  _____

  _____

Your Premarital Journal

What thoughts, ideas, decisions and prayer points would you like to keep a record of after reading this part of the manual? Write them in the space below:

PRINCIPLE #7

LEARN TO FUNCTION AS A TEAM

Two are better than one, because they have a good reward for their labour. For if they fall, one will lift up his companion. But woe to him who is alone when he falls, for he has no one to help him up. (Ecclesiastes 4:9-10.)

Marriage is teamwork. The two of you become one flesh. Your future and your destinies intertwine. Your missions and visions overlap. And your roles and responsibilities interlace. There is no getting away from the incredible teamwork that is required to merge these competing areas of your life into a productive whole.

Agree On Your Marriage Boundaries.

One of the first things you'll need to do is agree on your boundaries or your red lines, so to speak. I remember having that discussion with my wife when we began our journey. These are three things we agreed to work on from the very beginning.

1.) We agreed to pattern our lives after the principles and values we see in the Bible.

2.) We agreed never to threaten each other with divorce.

3.) We agreed never to raise our hands to hit or abuse each other.

After setting these boundaries, we prayed together for the grace we needed to observe and achieve them. That was over 42 years ago! Today, I can honestly say that neither one of us has ever broken those three values we agreed to live by.

As you start out your marriage journey, I want to encourage you to do something similar. Sit down and agree on what type of future you wish to arrive at, and take it to God in prayer together. If you can't both do that, you are probably not ready to get married.

Create Time For Team-working Exercises.

The second thing I want to encourage you to do is to create ample time to do several team-working exercises. In the early part of your relationship, you want to get a feel for how well you both work together —so that nothing catches you by surprise after you get married.

Too often when people are in love, they spend all their time going out and doing fun things romantically. While this is to be encouraged, it is more important that you create time to work at bonding in other areas of life. For instance, if you bond romantically, but not emotionally, intellectually or educationally—you will have big problems.

A series of team-building exercises may be what you need to see how compatible you really are. If you discover that you are both very different in certain areas, at least you will be aware of it; and you have a chance to talk about it, and perhaps get some counselling or coaching on how to deal with it.

That said, here are **8 suggestions** of things you can agree to do together, while you are dating or courting.

1. Practice Working on a Project Together:

This could be painting a room, helping a charity or assembling some furniture. Assign roles based on your strengths or preferences, and evaluate how well you both contribute to the success of the project. At the end, create time to discuss how you both felt it went and what you learnt about each other.

2. Practice Problem-Solving Scenarios:

If either of you is experiencing a challenge in an area of your life or career, agree to brainstorm together, to come up with ideas to solve or alleviate that problem. If you don't have a real challenge to discuss, you can discuss a hypothetical one. Something that can realistically happen in your future. The goal is to see how well you both communicate, collaborate, strategise, negotiate and deal with problems.

3. Practice Setting Goals together:

Spend an afternoon discussing and writing down some of your short-term or long-term goals as a couple. This might include setting goals for your relationship development, career, savings or raising funds for your wedding ceremony or your honeymoon. The goal of this exercise is to help you develop trust and the habit of discussing important issues together in the future.

4. Practice Weekly Reviews:

Try to schedule weekly appointments to discuss the week's highlights (whether positive or negative), plan future schedules, and table any pressing concerns. This exercise helps you both to stay connected and aware of what is happening in other areas of your life. It helps you develop a deeper understanding and empathy for each other; and creates opportunities to address concerns before they escalate.

5. Practice Communication Exercises:

Communication is such a major part of any relationship. So it makes sense to practice good communication skills. For instance, if you know that you are not a good listener, you can purposely set a timer (say, for 5 minutes) when your partner is speaking. You can tell your partner that you are doing this to help you listen to them without interrupting. When the timer goes off, you can volunteer to paraphrase what you heard and ask your partner to confirm that you heard them correctly. For fun, you can even switch roles. If you both do this, you will be sharpening your communication skills and developing disciplines that would benefit you both in other works of life.

6. Practice Expressing Gratitude:

It's very easy to take the people you see every day for granted. We love them, but quickly forget what they bring to our lives. That's why more than half of all married couples feel their spouses take them for granted. That said, establish a daily or weekly routine where you both agree to express something you appreciate about each other. This exercise will make it easier to nurture a sense of positive acceptance and emotional connection within your relationship both now and in the future.

7. Practice Doing Healthy Things Together:

When people fall in love, they tend to go out together to eat, watch movies and sit to talk. That's great, but try to fit in some health boosting activities too. Choose some physical activities you both enjoy, like jogging, biking, mountain climbing or walking. Then set a regular schedule for these activities. This exercise will not only help you maintain a healthy lifestyle, but will create fun memories that last a lifetime.

8. **Practice Budgeting Together:**

Another fun activity you can do together is to create a monthly budget; even if it is only a make-belief budget based on your present financial status. Here is what you can do. Imagine that you are getting married in 6 months, and need to make sure that your present income can cover your combined expenses, debts, and saving goals. Make out a detailed budget sheet separately, and then come together to compare how you've both allocated funds. Are your individual financial aims and goal closely aligned? Are there areas of your spending that can be better allocated? Are there challenges that need to be discussed and ironed out before you get married? Either way, this exercise will start to help you talk about your future and get over any financial awkwardness that can plague young couples.

In Conclusion:

If you endeavour to incorporate these exercises (or similar ones) into your routine while you are dating or courting, you will strengthen your relationship and develop a strong culture of teamwork. These activities will not only enhance your communication and problem-solving skills—but foster understanding, trust and mutual respect. You will find yourselves better able to navigate challenges and conflicts. And you will accommodate each other's needs with more empathy and understanding.

COUPLES DISCUSSION POINTS

- What are the lessons you are taking away from this principle?

  _____

  _____

  _____

- Choose any three suggestions above and decide to put them into practice over the next three weeks. Choose who will initiate it and when.

  _____

  _____

  _____

Your Premarital Journal

What thoughts, ideas, decisions and prayer points would you like to keep a record of after reading this part of the manual? Write them in the space below:

PRINCIPLE #8

PREPARE TO ADJUST YOUR DECISION-MAKING STYLE

As the Scriptures say, "A man leaves his father and mother and is joined to his wife, and the two are united into one." (Ephesians 5:31.) NLT.

When you get married, you are no longer two individuals but one. That means for every decision you wish to make, you are going to have to think about how it would affect your partner because you now share a life together. This shift requires a more collaborative approach to ensure that your needs and goals are both considered and addressed.

If you are both believers, the connection is even deeper because you both share in the mystical union of being in Christ. Your money is no longer just yours, it belongs to both of you. Your time is no longer for you to do what you like. You now have someone else to consider. Even your body is no longer just yours—it is to be shared with your spouse from the day you get married.

In 1 Corinthians chapter 7, Paul gives married couples the following advice:

> **"Let the husband render to his wife the affection due her, and likewise also the wife to her husband. The wife does not have authority over her own body, but the husband does. And likewise, the husband does not have authority over his own body, but the wife does."**
>
> (1 Corinthians 7:3-4.)

This is the way God set up the marriage institution. That being the case, the way you make decisions has to harmonise. For that to happen, you need to reflect on the following decision-making principles carefully:

1. Be Open and Honest.

To make good-to-great decisions, you must learn to be open and honest with each other. Share your thoughts, feelings, and preferences openly and boldly. Guard against being dishonest or immoral because the moment trust is broken, it's difficult to put it back together again.

2. Be Guided by your Shared Values.

Make sure your decisions align with your values and goals. For example, let's say one of your core values is to live debt-free, but you wish to buy a newer car since the old one is about to pack up. The particular vehicle you want will cause you to take on a large debilitating debt. To be true to this principle means that you'd have to agree to buy something cheaper for now, so that your core value is maintained.

3. Exercise Respect and Empathy.

Respect your spouse's opinions and perspectives, even if it's very different from your own. When you do your best to understand your partner's feelings and viewpoints, you show him or her that you respect their contribution to the marriage; and they are more likely to respect yours too.

4. Strive for Equality and Fairness.

Work hard to be fair to your partner. Avoid dominating the conversation or decision-making process. Even if your partner is the quiet type, insist on equal participation in decision-making. Ensure that you hear your spouse's contribution, and be sure to thank them for any suggestions they make.

5. Learn to Compromise.

Healthy decision-making usually requires some measure of healthy compromise. Many times you will need to find a middle ground. You'll need to look for thoughtful solutions that can meet both of your needs. At other times, you may need to agree to one partner's suggestion or solution if both are equally viable. It's okay if that happens occasionally; just try to make sure that the next time a similar situation occurs, the other partner's suggestion is tried.

6. Exercise Patience.

Take your time to make important decisions because they can make or break you. Allow time for both of you to think and express yourselves. Remember that some people can make decisions much quicker than others. So be patient with each other knowing that reaching an agreeable consensus might take time.

7. Be Adaptable and Flexible.

Sometimes the decision you might need to take may come from a third party. So, be open to asking for other people's input. For instance, there was a time I didn't know how to handle a certain challenge I was facing. When I spoke to a friend about it, the first suggestion he gave was exactly what I needed to do. Be prepared to consider other options, especially when they are coming from people who are more experienced than you.

Conclusion:

Be prepared to revisit and adjust your decision if the circumstances change or the actions you took don't work. Be Accountable to each other and take responsibility for your role in the process—whether it turns out good or not. Once you both made a decision, work hard to action it, even if the idea didn't come originally from you. Why? Because you are on the same team.

I am fully persuaded that if you and your spouse would embrace and apply these principles—that lead to better decision-making—they would help you foster an effective and harmonious partnership. Isn't that what marriage is all about?

Your Premarital Journal

What thoughts, ideas, decisions and prayer points would you like to keep a record of after reading this part of the manual? Write them in the space below:

PRINCIPLE #9

GENEROSITY LEADS TO SEXUAL INTIMACY

Let the husband render to his wife the affection due her, and likewise also the wife to her husband. The wife does not have authority over her own body, but the husband does. And likewise the husband does not have authority over his own body, but the wife does. Do not deprive one another except with consent for a time, that you may give yourselves to fasting and prayer; and come together again so that Satan does not tempt you because of your lack of self-control. (1 Corinthians 7:3-5.)

Many married couples struggle to achieve real sexual intimacy because they've never been shown how. They never saw it modelled consistently by the parental figures in their lives either. So, most of what we know about sexual intimacy comes from TV soaps and romantic movies—from the make-believe heart of Hollywood or Bollywood.

The problem is that most of these entertainment caricatures, are a far cry from real life. As a result, many couples enter into marriage without learning how to prepare for some of the main challenges that sex can bring up when the couple don't know what they are doing. I'm convinced that God gave us the beautiful gift of sex because He wants us to enjoy it. But it requires some learning.

In First Corinthians chapter 7, Paul's teaching on marital harmony paints the perfect picture of what should happen in every Christian marriage if we take God's Word seriously. Paul writes, **"Let the husband render to his wife the affection due her, and likewise also the wife to her husband."**

To render due affection in this passage means to give your spouse the quality of affection the person you love deserves—knowing that they have no other options or alternatives. Here we see a picture of a husband and his wife working diligently together to render affection to each other (not just during their honeymoon) but throughout their married life.

But what would motivate you to do this?

Answer: The realisation that God wants you to serve each other is the motivation. The understanding that God wants you and your partner to give pleasure to each other and to meet each other's sexual needs. The key to this kind of commitment is generosity! That's what your marriage vow is all about. It's about being intentionally generous to each other.

At some point, you will both promise to **serve** each other for the rest of your lives. That only works if you choose to be generous. So, understand that your marriage is a chance to **deliver** on that vow. I want you to know that when you get married, your sex life can go from good to better to best—as you mature.

If you learn to be generous and intimate, sex can be like wine. It can get better and sweeter with age. I'll say that again: Your sex life can get better and sweeter as you mature and learn to be more generous to each other. You can enjoy the precious gift of sex that God has given you both to enjoy.

Where to Start.

Here are three decisions I want you to start with—as you prepare yourself for a love life filled with passion, intimacy and joy.

1.) Embrace a Biblical View of Sex.

There is a Hollywood view of sex that is polar opposite to God's view. Paul alludes to God's view of sex when he wrote, **"Marriage is honourable among all, and the marriage bed is undefiled..."** (Hebrews 13:4.) Now the word **'undefiled'** used in this passage means pure, lovely, wholesome and beautiful. So, we learn two things about marriage and sex from this passage.

Firstly, that marriage is an honourable institution. Meaning it is to be regarded and respected as reputable and distinguished.

Secondly, that sex within marriage is not dirty, unclean or defiled. In other words, sex in marriage is pure, lovely, wholesome and beautiful.

Furthermore, sex is not just for **procreation**. It is designed to **lubricate** your marriage as well. And just like the engine oil you put in your vehicle, sex is designed to reduce **friction** and **heat** in your relationship. Sex also helps to **strengthen** your relationship and re-establish **emotional** connection.

Sex is a spiritual **service** husbands and wives are called to **render** to each other. When we generously and sensitively **make love**, we give each other a gift of joy, delight and pleasure. In marriage, sex is not just a **physical** act, it is a **spiritual** act too. When you make love—which to me is another way of saying you have sex in a truly loving way—you reaffirm your marriage **vows** and strengthen your marriage **covenant**.

This is how I felt the Holy Spirit explained it to me years ago. He said, **"When you pray, you commune with me spiritually; when you make love to your spouse, you commune with her spiritually too."** No wonder Paul called it a great mystery!

Here is what I want you to keep in your mind. Your marriage bed is where both of you proactively and unselfishly seek to **satisfy** each other. It is where you both seek to give pleasure and delight to each other. And, it is where the two of you seek to **serve** each other, lovingly and sacrificially. Nothing can be more beautiful.

If you understand and embrace these truths as a couple, your sex life will become more satisfying and more enjoyable. Sex will not be a chore you endure, but a priceless gift you lovingly and thoughtfully give to your only partner for life.

2. Resist the temptation to put your interest first.

Sex and selfishness don't go together. Why? Because sex, by definition, is a **selfless** act. The moment either party becomes selfish or self-centred, sex can quickly become strained or abusive. The truth is that real sexual intimacy only happens when you choose to lovingly serve your spouse.

When one partner is acting selfishly or uncaringly, the other partner always feels unloved, unappreciated or hurt. A distraught wife once said to me, "When my husband treats me badly and then demands for sex, I feel like a harlot after he has had his way with me." How sad is that? She didn't feel wanted or loved. She only felt used!

Intimacy happens when you choose to think more of the other person than you think of yourself. Hear me clearly, selfishness suffocates intimacy, openness, and sexual fulfilment. That's why Paul wrote, **"Let the husband render to his wife the affection due her (or owed to her), and likewise also the wife to her husband."**

He was saying that couples owe a '**debt**' (based on their marriage vows) that they must be eager to pay each other. That debt is '**affection**'. That debt is a willingness to serve and fulfil your partner's desire for intimacy.

Another lesson I learnt several years ago, is that God would sometimes leverage our sex life to **teach** us how to serve and love each other. Wow! I'll say that again: God would sometimes leverage your sex life to **teach** you how to serve and love your spouse. What I mean is that God may not remove the sexual challenges you have in your marriage until you learn to be more selfless.

When you come to see sex as God sees it—that is, as a character moulding tool in God's hands—it's easy to see why Paul would discourage couples from depriving each other of this amazing gift.

Do not deprive one another except with consent for a time, that you may give yourselves to fasting and prayer; and come together again so that Satan does not tempt you because of your lack of self-control. (1 Corinthians 7:5.)

3. Know that you can find the key to your spouse's passion if you search for it diligently.

I sometimes hear men say things like, "I don't know what makes my wife happy." My reply is usually, "Have you asked her?". Have you sat her down and said, "My darling wife, I love you so much and can't stand to see you unhappy or unfulfilled with our sexual life. Tell me what I can do or stop doing, to make things better." "Tell me how to love and cherish you like nobody else can."

I guarantee that if you would sincerely ask your spouse these type of questions, you will get very good answers that can start a process of healing and recovery. Everyone has something that turns them on, unlocks their passion or makes them come alive. It is your duty to find what that thing is. No matter how long it takes stay with it, because everyone's passion can be unlocked.

For some people, it's being affirmed, or receiving help, or feeling loved, or acts of random kindness. For others it's holidays, or hotel rooms, or massages, or beautiful flowers, or receiving domestic help. The important thing is to discover what makes your spouse tick and to make it happen as often as you can without going over the top.

Solomon's lover captured this concept well when she said:

> **"He brought me to the banqueting house, and his banner over me was love. He sustains me with cakes of raisins, and refreshes me with apples, for I am lovesick. His left hand is under my head, and his right-hand embraces me."** (Songs of Solomon 2:4.)

What was Solomon's lover saying in this text?

Solomon's lover was saying, "My lover knows me very well. He knows what I like. He knows how I like it. He knows how to refresh me and touch my sweet spot. He knows how to treat me well—and how to turn me on." Wow! What a great lover he was!!

Can your spouse say the same thing about you? If not, why not? If you've ever read the book of Songs of Solomon, you know that the man Solomon was a romantic. That tells me that all men can be romantic to some extent—if we choose to learn how. Sadly, too many men choose to believe the lie that they are not romantic.

Here is what I want to say to you as a man: There is a treasure waiting to be found in your spouse's garden. It's precious, valuable and beautiful, but it will stay hidden from you until you make a decision to find it. This usually takes a lot of time and effort, but the reward is so worth it. When you find your spouse's sweet spot, and when you find what makes her tick sexually, you have found the elusive fountain of marriage pleasure.

Let's talk about the practical stuff.

If you want to cultivate sexual intimacy you'll have to align the way you think with the way God thinks about the gift of sex He gave us. A lot of the things I will say here apply to both sexes. But I will say that some things may apply more to one sex than the other.

Advice To Ladies

1. View Sex as an Act of Worship.

A disproportionate number of women say they find sex a tad bit tedious, to put it lightly. That can change if they see it as an extension of their worship. As a matter of fact, everything we do as Christians is an act of worship to God. And sex is not excluded from the list.

Sex is not just a sensual act, it is a spiritual act too. It's our reasonable service, both to God who gave it to us, and to our spouse who we **serve** in this beautiful way. In Colossians 3:17, the Bible says: **"And whatever you do in word or deed, do all in the name of the Lord Jesus, giving thanks to God the Father through Him."**

Verse 23 says,

> **"And whatever you do, do it heartily, as to the Lord and not to men."**

The purpose of sex is more than the act of enjoying each other. It is a sacred and priceless gift you give to your spouse. If you see sex in this way, you will find it much more pleasurable and desirable. In addition, you will **serve** it lovingly to your spouse in ways that delight or enthral them—and glorify the Lord.

2. Understand that your husband doesn't just want sex, he needs it.

Too many ladies are tempted to think that all a man wants is sex. But that's not true. Men don't just want sex, they need it. Why is that?

a.) **Sex affirms a man's manhood in ways that are too deep to articulate in this book.** But I will say that sex enhances your man's self-esteem, in the same way as positive and affirming words build yours.

b.) **Sex gratifies a man's innermost desire to be close and**

intimate with his wife. A man feels abandoned, forsaken and rejected when his sexual needs are not met. That's why I said, men need sex.

c.) **Sex helps a man to forgive, forget and heal**—especially after he feels disrespected or dishonoured. Why do I say that? Because sex puts his mind at rest. That may be why men fall asleep easily after having sex. You could say that sex is like an Anaesthetic for men. He needs it to heal, to rest and to reset.

In short, ladies need to know that good sex is a man's emotional Oxygen. His emotional tank is refreshed, refilled, and refuelled by it. So if you starve a healthy married man of sex, you will 'kill' him emotionally—and in several other ways too.

3. Realise that sex is actually good for you.

Yes, it is. It's a medically proven fact. Several years ago, I came across a report from a survey that was done on women who claimed to be 'sexually satisfied'. I wrote down some of the main conclusions of the report, but can't remember the source. Here are some of the conclusions as I penned them:

- Good sex will make you a happier woman, because you have a happier and more fulfilled husband.
- Good sex will make you look and feel younger, stronger, and sexier. It is even found to produce better glowing skin.
- Sex helps to stimulate and produce endorphins and Anti-bodies—which in turn will help to improve your general health.
- Good sex reduces stress and stress related ailments—like high blood pressure and diabetes.
- Regular sex strengthens the heart, as it is a form of exercise.
- Good sex will make your husband less likely to stray or be tempted to use pornography—especially as he ages.

4. Learn to treat sex the same way you treat food.

I learnt this from a friend many years ago. He said sex is like **food**. Sometimes, when you are not very hungry, you go for a **snack**. At other times you may want a **proper meal**. Then, there are those occasions when you want a **5-course feast**.

Well, that's how sex is, especially for men. Sometimes all your spouse needs is a quick **snack**. A snack (in sex terms) represents a quick release. This generally happens when one of you is turned on, but you only have a few minutes to make love. Well, go for it! I know someone who likes to call it a **'quickie'**. He often joked and said, "I feel so energised after my wife and I have had a quickie."

Sometimes you may have half an hour to spend together—say, in the evenings after a long day's work. We call this type of sex, a **meal**. You have a bit more time to kiss, cuddle, and make love. The purpose of a meal (in sex terms) is to reconnect with each other. To lubricate your relationship. And, to create a rhythm of connectedness. If you are younger, this might happen two to five times a week depending, of course, on several factors.

At other times, you and your spouse might take a weekend away or travel to an exotic place to be together. Presumably, you have all the time in the world to enjoy each other. You have time for a spa, a jacuzzi bath, or a hot massage. You may even have access to the Presidential Suite with a Queen-sized bed. This is not your everyday sex, so I call it a **feast**.

Here is the point. Variety is the spice of life! And variety is healthy for your marriage. So, I encourage you to try different things when you get married. Keep your sex life ticking during hectic seasons of life with a **quickie** or a **meal**. But also make time for those amazing **feasts** that feel like heaven on earth.

When you prioritise your sex life, it will help to soothe away most of the stones life throws at you. It will mitigate against conflict, stress, and burnout. Let the aim of your lovemaking be to serve each other, to give pleasure to each other, and to give the **gift** of true love to the love of your life.

5. Don't hesitate to explore different sexual positions.

There is no one way to make love. How you have sex is entirely up to the two of you. That's why good communication is so necessary. You have to talk. You have to explain to your spouse how you want him or her to treat you. Why? Because sex is meant to be enjoyed, not endured.

The missionary position is great, but there are other sex positions or styles that can be more comfortable during certain seasons of life. In saying this, I'm not suggesting that you practice any form of **nasty** sex. No, you are a Christian. That means your sexual preferences need to be lawful, not inappropriate, dirty, or sex that makes you uncomfortable.

Being a Christian doesn't mean you must settle for a boring sex life. God wants you to have a blast with your spouse. That's why He gave you this amazing gift. King Solomon put it this way. He said:

> **"Drink water from your own cistern, and running water from your own well. Let your fountain be blessed, and rejoice with the wife of your youth. As a loving deer and a graceful doe, let her breasts satisfy you at all times; and always be enraptured with her love."** (Proverbs 5:15, 18, 19.)

Solomon was teaching us to enjoy our sex life and make sure we are satisfied when we make love. Your cistern is a reservoir of pleasure, not of boredom. If you make the right allowances for each other, serve each other, forgive each other and love each other like Christ loves you; your gift of sex will make you very grateful and very happy.

Advice To Men:

I often hear people say that ladies determine the atmosphere in the home. That may be true in some areas, but when it comes to sex, I am convinced that men determine the atmosphere. Men can do a whole lot more to improve the sex quotient of the marriage. Why do I say this? I say it because men are the leaders and heads of their homes.

So, here are a few bits of advice for men:

1. Understand your wife's definition of intimacy, because it's likely to be different from yours.

Most men feel intimate with their spouses when they are having sex. So for most men, sex equals intimacy. But that's seldom the case for women. Most women see intimacy as what men say or do before they jump into bed. I will dare to say that the majority of women I know, need to feel that sense of closeness that comes from a gentle touch, a long warm hug, a romantic walk in the park, a heartwarming talk, nonsexual caresses, a bunch of beautiful flowers, or a box of delightful chocolates.

As a man, you need to find out what your wife's definition of intimacy looks like, so you can be on the same page with her sexually. This is because in general, it takes a woman longer to feel ready for sex than it takes a man.

2. Know that ladies are like flowers, they open up sexually when the atmosphere is ideal.

Atmosphere, ambience, environment, privacy, conditions, mood, feelings, harmony, and circumstances. These are all words that describe how most ladies judge the timing of sex. If a woman is anxious, worried or unhappy, sex can feel like a **chore**, no matter how much she loves it.

Once a man is turned on, he can have sex at the drop of a hat; but it's not that simple with most women. They thrive better when their environment is warm, peaceful and beautiful. Most women are at their sexiest when they feel loved, cherished, protected, secured, and wooed. Therefore it's a man's duty to work hard to make the home a loving and peaceful safe space.

What can you do to make that happen? Be gentle with your lady. Be kind. Be understanding. Deal with conflict speedily. Reaffirm your unfailing love to your spouse regularly. Reassure her of your commitment to her wellbeing by your words and (more importantly), by your actions. Don't forget to help out around the home as well—because women generally tend to find it sexy.

3. Understand that every part of a lady's life is interconnected to every other part.

A woman's psychology, physiology, anatomy and neurology are all wonderfully intertwined. If something is bothering her, it will tend to affect every other area of her life. Men, on the other hand, are much better at compartmentalising their lives. Generally, if a man is stressed at work, he can leave his stress in the office, and still enjoy sex with his wife when he gets home. Why? Because sex is therapy for a man.

Women, on the other hand, find it difficult to be so surgical. If they are stressed at work, eight out of ten times, it will feature in one form or the other, in the home or bedroom. Many women find it difficult to relax and enjoy sex if something is bothering them.

What can you as a man do about it? You can create time to talk about what is bothering her. The mere fact that you are sensitive to her need, is sometimes more than enough to turn the tide. Once she unburdens and receives your empathy, the feelings will follow—all things being equal. I like to say it this way: A happy woman is a sexy woman.

4. Learn to see sex as the icing on the cake, and everything you do before sex as 'baking the cake'.

If the ingredients you use to make your 'cake' are bad, no amount of icing will make it enjoyable. It's important to remember that love-making does not start in the bedroom for a lady. It starts 24 to 48 hours before the sex act. It was either brewing all day long or it was being poisoned.

That caring text you sent to your spouse at lunch yesterday. That reassuring word you gave her before she went in to present her ideas to her boss. The dishes you decided to load into the dishwasher. All these little ways of affirming your spouse and showing her that you care about her and what she is going through; are all preparation and ingredients for what I like to call, **'good-to-great' sex.**

Sadly, too many men don't know this secret about their wives. So they go for the icing before they get around to baking the cake; so to speak. It's important that your wife feels valued and cherished for her to open up completely. Anything less is likely to make her feel like a sex object. Believe me, no respectable lady wants to be a sex toy.

The Apostle Paul encapsulated this principle perfectly well when he wrote, **"Let the husband render to his wife the affection due her..."** (1 Corinthians 7:3.). I've discovered that there is an amount of affection every woman needs to prepare her for meaningful and mutually enjoyable sex.

5. Ladies are like the Electric Cookers, they take time to get going.

I once heard a preacher say, *"Men are like Gas Stoves, they are piping hot in 10 seconds. Ladies, on the other hand, are like*

Electric Cookers, they take time to get going."

I heard this saying several years ago—before modern electric cookers (that get red hot in 15 seconds) were common. But this quotation made sense to me because when I was growing up in the '60s and '70s, you had to wait for 3 to 4 minutes to get your cooking going on the electric hobs we had in those days.

The point the preacher was making is that men get turned on and off fairly quickly and easily, but women need time to get into the mood. So as a man, you'll need to learn her mood. You'll need to be romantic, be patient, discover her sweet spot, take your time, caress her where it matters, and hold back ejaculating prematurely during sex.

Why are these things important? They are important because most women need more time to reach their peak. And that includes orgasm. It takes a mature, unselfish man, to care about his wife more than he cares about himself; but it's very doable!

Ask the Lord to help you figure out the woman He so graciously gave to you. God knew you both have the wisdom and the desire to figure each other out. That's why He paired you up in His Sovereign wisdom. So don't get tired of studying your spouse and asking her what she prefers, until you know her likes and dislikes intimately. Until you know what makes her tick and what makes her alarm go off—if you know what I mean.

One last thing I wish to mention here is that a few people (both male and female) struggle with sex for any number of reasons. Sometimes, it's connected to how they were introduced to sex in the first place. Was it abusive or a source of pain and regret? At other times, the problem can come from any number of medical diagnosable conditions. If your spouse has any of these challenges, don't be ashamed to seek medical, psychological, or spiritual help.

It's amazing how easily and quickly some of these sexual issues can be resolved. So don't suffer in silence. Don't be like a lady I know, who frustrated her husband and avoided sex for the first 5 or 6 years of their marriage. She did so because it was painful for her. But once she got a diagnosis and was treated, the issue subsided drastically.

Talk to your doctor as soon as you sense something might be wrong. If its source is spiritual, talk to your pastor or someone who can counsel and pray with you. Jesus said: **"And you shall know the truth, and the truth shall make you free."** (John 8:32.).

So, do whatever it takes to be free from the effects of your past. And remember, God gave us the **gift** of sex for our continuous enjoyment. Don't let ignorance, shame, or embarrassment keep you from enjoying it with your partner.

COUPLES DISCUSSION POINTS

- What lessons are you taking away from this principle?

  _____

  _____

  _____

  _____

- If either of you has been sexually active in the past but hasn't talked about it in detail, find some time today or later in the week to talk frankly about it. It's important that you both come clean—because no one likes to be surprised by historical sex-related issues after the wedding.

  _____

  _____

  _____

Your Premarital Journal

What thoughts, ideas, decisions and prayer points would you like to keep a record of after reading this part of the manual? Write them in the space below:

PRINCIPLE #10

KNOW THE IN-LAWS AND THE OUT-LAWS

"Pursue peace with all people, and holiness, without which no one will see the Lord." (Hebrews 12:14.)

One of the most challenging aspects of marriage is that when you marry a person, you are invariably marrying into their family. Whether you like it or not, your spouse's family are your in-laws. In-laws generally love to be involved in the life of their family members and it is not always wrong for them to do so.

What matters is how you and your spouse handle the challenges that can arise from the different personalities involved. Fortunately, there are healthy things you can do to reduce conflict and improve your relationship with them. Here is a list of key considerations for you and your spouse to keep in mind when relating to in-laws:

1.) Be intentional about trying to build a good relationship with your in-laws.

No matter how troublesome your in-laws may appear to be, God loves them. That means you must try to love them too. You can't force them to change, but your attitude towards them can influence the way they think or respond to you. If you build a good relationship with your in-laws, you can reduce tension and build mutual respect. One way to do that is by finding common interests or activities to share with them. And, this could be with or without the involvement of your spouse.

2.) Agree on how you would respond to issues with the in-laws before you get married.

Honouring your parents does require that you show them kindness, patience, gentleness, and respect. This applies to in-laws as well. You may not even like them, but you need to choose to act in a loving manner towards them. If they feel that you honour and respect them, they are more likely to honour and respect you as well.

That said, here are three principles that can help you come up with a strategy you can both agree on:

1.) **Agree not to air your marital troubles or challenges to your parents or in-laws.** At least not initially. If you report each other to your parents or in-laws when things are tough, they may form a negative opinion of your spouse that never goes away, even when things are good between you. That's dangerous! Every marriage will have its challenges, learn to walk through them together. If you are still having major challenges, get help from an impartial counsellor or minister—who is not a family member.

[*Having said that, there may be two exceptions to this principle. The **first** is if your relatives are **spiritually mature**, capable of giving you unbiased counsel, and you both agree that they are the best people to help you through the challenges.*

*The **second** exception is where serious **physical, mental or sexual abuse** is happening in your marriage. You may have to speak to someone in the family who can step in to stop the abuse. I pray that this would never happen to you.*]

This might be a great time to hold hands and vow never to physically, emotionally, verbally or sexually abuse each other. So help you God!

2.) **Challenging discussions with your family should be initiated and led by you—not by your spouse.** If a member of your family is meddling or overreaching in your affairs, you should be the one to confront or speak to them on behalf of your new family. Your family are more likely to respect your desires and opinions than your spouse's desires and opinions. If your spouse is forced to challenge their behaviour, they may see him or her as controlling and disrespectful. But if you step up and cover your spouse, they would most likely see the unity between you and step back. The same concept should be practised the other way around.

3.) **Never talk to in-laws or family about issues without first agreeing on a clear position with your spouse.** Family and in-laws can be very good at exploiting any division between you and your spouse, so it is very important that you are singing from the same script. For instance, your family may want you to contribute some money for a project that is important to them. They may speak to you and expect you to make a commitment there and then. **Don't do it!** Instead, tell them that you will discuss the issue with your spouse and get back to them. The goal is to always present a united front to your family and in-laws.

3.) Establish sensible boundaries as early as possible.

Another important thing to do when relating to family and in-laws is to set clearly defined boundaries. Boundaries help prevent conflict and misunderstandings. Discuss and agree on what is or isn't acceptable regarding your in-law's involvement in your lives. For instance, how would you handle uninvited opinions or advice? How would you deal with unreasonable pressure to start having children nine months after you get married?

Another common example is that your family may expect your new family to spend every Christmas with them. After all, that has always been the family tradition. How would you lovingly and respectfully say no—especially if you need to explore other options—like spending the day with your spouse's family? These and many other issues will come up, and when they do, you need to know when to compromise and when to stand your ground.

Some of these decisions can be a little easier if you've already talked about them and set some boundaries. God knew that close family members would still want to advise and influence their grown-up children. That may be why He inspired this powerful picture of the marriage institution right from the start: **"Therefore a man shall leave his father and mother and be joined to his wife, and they shall become one flesh."** (Genesis 2:24.) The goal of marriage is to move away from the influence of family—and become one with your spouse. Never forget that!

4.) Agree to always present a united front

before your in-laws.

Consistency between you and your spouse ensures that in-laws do not exploit perceived weaknesses in your relationship. No matter what you are going through as a couple, agree to be united when dealing with family. If not, they will play a game of 'divide and conquer' with you. For example, if you say one thing to your family and your spouse says something completely different, they are going to see one of you as the bad cop and the other as the good cop. So, it's crucial to discuss and agree on your responses or decisions privately before presenting them to your family or in-laws.

5.) If your family are the cause of misunderstanding or conflict, you should take the lead in dealing with it.

We touched on this concept above, but it bears repeating here. You certainly understand your family better than your spouse does—and vice versa. Your spouse may find it more difficult to understand and deal with your family issues. So, you have to **bravely** step up and step in whenever there is an issue to handle with your family.

You can both soften the blow on your relationship by gently educating each other on the unique histories and idiosyncrasies of your families. If you do, you will both find it easier to handle challenges with empathy, because you better understand what is at play behind the scenes.

6.) Choose your battles wisely.

There are too many little things that can cause conflict between you and your in-laws. Try not to pick on every small issue that arises. If you restrain yourself from constantly bringing up irritating issues, when the big things happen and you bring it to their attention, they are more likely to take you seriously. But if you bring up every little issue you are not happy with, they would just see you as a negative, confrontational and hyper-sensitive killjoy.

Focus instead on what truly matters to your family and avoid constantly arguing with them over insignificant things. For instance, if your mother-in-law likes to rearrange things in your kitchen when she visits, but it doesn't really disrupt your daily life, it might be better to let it slide.

When these type of misunderstandings or challenges rear their ugly heads, try to see the situation from your in-laws's perspective as well. After all, if she is going to be doing the cooking, it shouldn't matter how she arranges the space she uses. Of course, you can always put things back when her visit is over. The goal is to maintain peace, which only requires one mature person. Let that person be you.

7.) Communicate with your in-laws openly and honestly.

Open communication prevents small issues from snowballing into larger ones. For instance, if an in-law says or does something that bothers you, discuss it with your spouse calmly—and decide the best way and time to deal with it. Ask yourselves these two questions.

1.) Was what they did intentionally done to dishonour or hurt you? If the answer is 'yes'—you may have to confront the behaviour as soon as possible. But if the answer is 'no'—it may be one of the things to overlook, because it's not a big deal.

2.) Is the issue you are concerned about, a red line that needs to be addressed or not? Only you and your spouse can make that decision. But if it has something to do with your values, your faith or your marriage harmony, I would suggest that you confront it or at least highlight it to them.

In the end, open communication is better than concealed anger. I know it's not always easy to deal with in-laws who are often older than you. But you have to find a way of stamping your preferences on the minds of your in-laws. Nevertheless, try to be understanding and respectful in doing so.

8.) Celebrate and appreciate your in-laws often.

In-laws are people—and people like to be appreciated. So, regularly think of creative ways to show your appreciation to your in-laws. You don't need to spend loads of money to do so, but (depending on their taste) you may need to put some money aside to get them a treat. For instance, just dropping a beautifully scented candle at your in-law's home for no particular reason (with a note saying, "Mum and Dad, We love and appreciate you!") may tip the scale in your favour for years to come.

Another way to show your love and appreciation to your in-laws is to always remember their birthdays, anniversaries, and special occasions. Send them a gift card, a bouquet of flowers, or a piece of custom jewellery. Even if you can't afford a gift, always take time out to call them. To wish them a Happy Anniversary or an uplifting day. It doesn't cost you anything to send them an appreciative text or a free E-card either. It all goes a long way to building goodwill and maintaining a healthy relationship with them.

9.) Take an interest in your in-law's unique culture, traditions, or customs.

Nine out of ten times, your in-laws would practice unique customs and traditions that you are not familiar with. Just because you didn't grow up with these traditions and customs doesn't make them bad or wrong. They are usually just different! If you are open to learning how other people live, you may discover a wealth of values or practices that can enhance and bring diversity into your new family life.

So, take an interest in the traditions, customs, values and stories that come from your partner's side of the family. Ask plenty of questions, so you can understand their unique perspectives. Be mindful that what might be considered polite or normal in your culture could be viewed differently by your in-laws—and vice versa. Take time to learn about these differences and respect them.

If some of those customs infringe on your Christian beliefs or values, respectfully tell them so, and excuse yourself from participating. It's better to upset them when it matters than to compromise your principles. From my experience, your in-laws will eventually come to respect you as a person of morals and principles, if you do things the right way.

COUPLES DISCUSSION POINTS

- What new lessons have you learnt from this principle?

  _____

  _____

  _____

- Agree on which one of these ideas you can start to roll out from now, to help you get closer to your in-laws.

  _____

  _____

  _____

Your Premarital Journal

What thoughts, ideas, decisions and prayer points would you like to keep a record of after reading this part of the manual? Write them in the space below:

PRINCIPLE #11

KEEP GOD AT THE CENTRE OF YOUR HOME AND MARRIAGE.

"Unless the LORD builds the house, they labour in vain who build it; Unless the LORD guards the city, the watchman stays awake in vain." (Psalm 127:1.)

Most people would define marriage as a union between a man and a woman. And although there is some truth in that definition, it is not a completely accurate definition. Biblically speaking, marriage is a covenant agreement between a man, a woman, and the God who saved them and brought them together. That means your marriage can never be as strong as it was designed to be if God is not an integral part of that union.

In fact, God is the only constant and unchanging one in the union. The man and wife may change; their circumstances may change; but God stays reliable and immutable. It was this threefold union that Solomon was referring to when he said, **"Three cords twisted together cannot be easily broken."** (Ecclesiastes 4:12.)

Solomon was teaching us that our marriages wouldn't fall apart so easily if God is recognised and honoured as the third and most significant partner in the relationship. Things will never really come together for your marriage like they should if you don't embrace this divine triangle.

Keeping God at the centre of your marriage implies that you will both need to embrace God's **leadership** in your home and in your dealings with each other. It means that you will agree not to take any important steps without coming to a joint agreement. It implies that you will choose to pray and study God's Word together and commit yourselves to obeying what it teaches.

Keeping God in the centre of your home also means that you would honour, respect and treat your spouse the way you would if Jesus Christ Himself **lived** in your home and **went** everywhere with you. In short, keeping God at the centre of your marriage is hard work. It can't be done with a nonchalant attitude and you wouldn't succeed unless you have a strong desire to **honour** God completely in your life and marriage.

Here are **seven** important things you must learn to do to keep God at the centre of your Marriage:

1. Find time to study the Bible and pray with your spouse regularly.

One of the lies your enemy tries to sell you is that you don't have enough time to do certain important things. But that is a lie. You always have time to do the things that are important to you. Praying and studying the Bible together is one of those important things that can suffer in marriage if care is not taken. But the spiritual health of your marriage depends on it.

If you don't already study your Bible together, I want to encourage you to start as soon as possible. You don't need to spend an hour initially. You can start by spending 10 or 15 minutes a day. If God is to remain at the centre of your marriage, He will need to instruct you and your spouse regularly. Studying the Bible and praying together is the most common way He does that.

Engaging with the Bible as a couple will enhance your spiritual, emotional, and relational well-being. It will provide valuable guidance and inspiration for your marriage journey as well. Schedule it if you must, but make sure that you do it, because your spiritual, emotional, and physical health really depends on it.

2. Practice the presence of God daily.

The phrase, '**practising the presence of God**' has been used for years in Christendom to describe the intentional act of worshipping, praying, or meditating about God—in order to stay connected with Him in a personal and ongoing way. God promised to reveal Himself to us when we take Him seriously. Through the prophet Jeremiah, He made us this promise:

> **"And you will seek Me and find Me, when you search for Me with all your heart."** (Jeremiah 29:13.)

To practice the presence of God is to cultivate a constant awareness of God's existence and involvement in your life. It is engaging in ongoing conversations with God, not just during designated times of Prayer or Bible Study, but during your daily chores and activities. It is being present with God in your thoughts and actions, and acknowledging His presence throughout the day.

When you practice the presence of God, you know that He is with you at all times, and you are confident that He's got your back. Practising the presence of God allows you to experience a profound and ongoing connection with God in all aspects of your life. And it helps to foster spiritual growth and a sense of inner peace and purpose daily.

When you seek God in this way, you can expect to sense God's powerful presence, hear His convicting voice and experience His overwhelming peace—no matter what is happening around you. Enoch was an example of a man who enjoyed God's presence so much that he was simply caught up into heaven, and no one ever found his body.

> **"Enoch walked faithfully with God; then he was no more, because God took him away."** (Genesis 5:24.)

God must have enjoyed walking and talking with Enoch, that He simply whisked him away. When you decide to focus your attention and thoughts on the presence of God, you will start to experience more of His presence. You will become more conscious and aware that the Almighty God is indeed with you and in you. And, your relationship with your spouse will reflect this new awareness. God's presence will help you put all of life into perspective, and you will get much better at dealing with the stresses of life.

Your capacity to keep God at the centre of your marriage will enlarge as you become more conscious of His presence in your life, home and marriage. If you or your spouse are learning this concept for the first time, I want to challenge you to pause now and agree on how you can adopt it into your lives. Here is what I know for sure, this one practice out weighs a hundred marriage improvement principles and strategies. So, start practising it today, and don't procrastinate.

3. Find a great Church and commit to diligently serving and contributing there.

If you want the presence and power of God in your home, you must honour God's instructions to stay connected to other like-minded Believers. Why? Because your faith was not designed to be practiced in isolation, but in fellowship with others. That's why the Bible says:

> **"And let us consider how to stir up one another to love and good works, not neglecting to meet together, as is the habit of some, but encouraging one another, and all the more as you see the Day drawing near."** (Hebrews 10:24-25.)

God designed the local Church to be a place where you can connect with a larger spiritual family. God knew that you would need such a family, where you can receive encouragement, support and instruction. He knew you would need a place to invest your gifts and talents, and to serve God and His people.

If you would commit to a good local Church together, you will not only experience more opportunities for spiritual growth and maturity, but find that the Church will aid you in your commitment to keep God at the centre of your home and marriage.

4. Develop friendships with people who are striving to go where you want to go in your life and marriage.

Another way of putting the is point is to aspire to make friends with people who are already achieving in their relationship, what you are aiming to achieve in yours. These people don't need to be perfect—since no one is perfect—but they need to be making positive progress in their relationships. They also need to be the type of people who don't compromise, quit or give up on their values.

"Evil company", they say, "corrupts good manners". But the opposite is also true. "Good company, influences us to be better people." It's important to watch the friendships you and your spouse keep, because they have a way of influencing you—positively or negatively. The Scripture expresses this truth well when it says:

"The righteous should choose his friends carefully, because the way of the wicked leads them astray." (Proverbs 12:26.)

If you really want to honour God and keep Him at the centre of your marriage, you will need to find people who are best suited to help you stay on course. You must be willing to invest in them (in any way you can), so that they may in turn be motivated to invest in you. You can do that by inviting them out to dinner—and paying for it. Or by volunteering to help them in some useful way.

If you both aim to maintain a circle of positive friendships that align with your values and support your well-being, those friends will be an amazing support system for your marriage. A wise counsellor once said, **"Show me your friends and I will show you your future"**. What he meant was that your friends and acquaintances will influence your destiny. If that is true (and I'm positive it is), you and your spouse must both aim to choose your friends wisely and prayerfully.

5. Schedule time to read inspirational books, listen to motivational talks, and watch uplifting movies or programmes together.

Most of us are bombarded daily with discouraging and de-motivating narratives. Whether it's from the morning news, the dreadful traffic, the annoying colleague at work, or the scores of life's setbacks, the outcome is the same. We are deflated, discouraged, or depressed by them all.

The things you feed your mind and spirit on are going to determine what priorities you embrace. So, if your priority is to keep God in the centre of your marriage, you will need to consume and focus more on spiritually uplifting soul food.

One of the ways to keep your marriage interesting and fresh is to read together, listen to something inspirational together, or watch something positive together. If you do, it will keep your mind sharp, improve your vocabulary, increase your knowledge, strengthen your analytical thinking faculties, and enhance your focus and concentration.

> "Finally, brethren, whatever things are true, whatever things are noble, whatever things are just, whatever things are pure, whatever things are lovely, whatever things are of good report, if there is any virtue and if there is anything praiseworthy--meditate on these things." (Philippians 4:8.)

6. Pepper your home with visible plaques, posters, pictures, artefacts, or drawings that reassure you of God's vital partnership in your marriage.

We often forget important things that should never be forgotten, because they are out of sight. That's why we usually write a list of things we want to do, buy, or not forget; and place it somewhere prominent so it's there to remind us. So, intentionally place things all around your home that continually remind you to keep God at the centre of your marriage. Whether it's a painting, a drawing, a picture or an artefact is not that important. What is important is that it jogs your memory and focuses your energies in the right direction. What you see around you can have a profound impact on your thoughts, emotions, and behaviour.

> "And these words which I command you today shall be in your heart... You shall bind them as a sign on your hand, and they shall be as frontlets between your eyes. You shall write them on the doorposts of your house and on your gates." (Deuteronomy 6:6,8,9.)

God instructed His people to put signs, tablets and plaques around their homes to remind them of His commandments because He knows how forgetful we can be. If you pepper your home, office or vehicle with reminders of what you are trying to achieve as a couple or family—they will keep your eyes on the prize.

7. Live each day by the principles of love.

If you and your spouse want the power of God in your home and marriage, you will need to let the love of God guide your actions and speech every day. Let me repeat that: If you and your spouse want the power of God in your home and marriage, you will need to let the love of God guide your actions and speech every day.

I know we all have our own favourite definition of love. But none of our definitions matter if they don't reflect God's perfect definition. This is how the Spirit of God defined it:

"Love suffers long and is kind; love does not envy; love does not parade itself, is not puffed up; does not behave rudely, does not seek its own, is not provoked, thinks no evil; does not rejoice in iniquity, but rejoices in the truth; bears all things, believes all things, hopes all things, endures all things. Love never fails." (1 Corinthians 13:4-8.)

The kind of love that works in the marriage institution is the type that never fails. The type that is truly kind, patient, considerate, sacrificial, and humble. It's the love that proceeds from God himself. That's why marriage doesn't work well for a Believer if God is not in the centre of it. The good news is that every true Christian has this God-kind of love.

Romans 5:5 says, **"...God's love has been poured into our hearts through the Holy Spirit who has been given to us."**

This means that you have a deposit of divine love in you. You can love your spouse with the God-kind of love. You can be kind. You can be considerate. You can care. You can make sacrifices. You can be patient with your spouse. It's all within your reach and your power.

If you just believe this, you will never again say, "**I can't do this**". Or, "**I don't love you any more.**" That's a lie from the pit of hell because the love of God is in your heart—and God's love never quits, falters or fails. We live in a world that minimises, devalues, trivialises and even scornes marriage; but that's because people have rejected God's immutable wisdom and have embraced man-made foolishness.

Nevertheless, a marriage based on God's principles and precepts is designed to be a shining light in a dark world. From experience, I can tell you that God loves to stay in the centre of any relationship that endeavours to exhibit true sacrificial love. Why? **Because God Himself is love.** (1 John 4:8.)

Pray for the grace to embrace these truths. I challenge you to love and care for your spouse, not because it is easy, but because it is your reasonable service. (See Romans 12:1-2.) Decide to change the narrative in your lineage, by embracing the grace of God that makes all things possible. If you do, it will be a win-win for you and your spouse, and for all those who look up to you as long as your live.

COUPLES DISCUSSION POINTS

- What new ideas have you learnt from this principle?

  _____

  _____

- Discuss how well you have kept God at the centre of your life till now. What can you both change to make His presence more tangible going forward?

  _____

  _____

Your Premarital Journal

What thoughts, ideas, decisions and prayer points would you like to keep a record of after reading this part of the manual? Write them in the space below:

CHAPTER 8

HOW TO ELIMINATE STRESS FROM YOUR WEDDING DAY

Be anxious for nothing, but in everything by prayer and supplication, with thanksgiving, let your requests be made known to God; and the peace of God, which surpasses all understanding, will guard your hearts and minds through Christ Jesus. (Philippians 4:6-7.)

Planning your wedding is going to be very exciting, and yet you are probably going to find some of it a bit stressful. To help ease the pressure and ensure that your special day is filled with great memories, here are 12 important things you and your spouse can do:

1. Consider getting a Wedding Planner.

I know getting a wedding planner is expensive. But if you can afford it, it may be worth the money if it takes a lot of the pressure off you. If you can't afford a wedding planner, delegate tasks to trustworthy friends and family members. Of course, you will have to trust that they can deliver, but most of your friends and family members are almost as invested in your wedding as you are. So, from experience, many of them will do their best for you. Delegating not only lightens your load, but allows others to feel involved in your big day.

2. Set a Realistic Budget.

One of the biggest stressors in wedding planning is money. By setting a clear, realistic budget from the outset, you avoid financial surprises and disagreements down the line. Ensure you factor in all expenses, including those little extras that often get overlooked. Here is a list of most of the things you will need to budget for. It's not exhaustive, but it will get you started.

Attire

- Wedding rings
- Tuxedo
- Groom's Shoes
- Tie and Cufflinks
- Wedding Dress
- Bridal Shoes
- Veil or Hair Accessories
- Jewellery
- Slip or Lingerie
- Alterations
- Change of Clothing

Venue
- Church Venue
- Reception Hall
- Dance Floor
- Hotel for Couple
- Officiating Minister(s)
- Ushers
- Reception Food Service
- Reception Drinks
- Wedding Cake(s)
- Cake Knife and Serving sets

Decorations
- Church Decor
- Reception Decor
- Reception Centre-pieces
- Bridal Bouquet
- Bridesmaids Bouquets
- Flower Girls Flowers
- Ringer Bearer's Pillow

Entertainment
- Pianist for the Church
- Soloist or Choir
- Band or DJ
- Master of Ceremony

Photos and Videos
- Engagement Photos & Video
- Wedding Day Photographer
- Wedding Day Videographer

Beauty
- Facials
- Hair Styling
- Manicure & Pedicure
- Makeup Service

- Hair Cut (for the Groom)

Transportation
- Limo for Couple
- Transport for Guests
- Transport for Bridal Train

Guests
- Save the Date Cards
- Invitations
- Wedding Program
- Reception Menus
- Table Cards
- Guest Book
- Wedding Favours
- Bridal Party Gifts
- Gifts for Parents
- Gifts for Groomsmen
- Gifts for Brides Maid & Best Man
- Thank you Card

Others
- Marriage Licence
- Marriage Certificate
- Wedding Planner/Coordinator

3. Reject Perfectionism and be Flexible.

Understand that wedding events happen with real people, not with inanimate things that can be staged perfectly. Not everything will go exactly as planned, and that's okay. If you understand this, you will not hold yourself to unrealistic expectations. Understand that perfection is an illusion, and be willing to adapt to changes without letting them ruin your day. Also, embrace the idea that whatever happens will make your wedding unique to you.

4. Refuse to Yield to External Pressures and Expectations.

Too many people make themselves slaves to societal norms and family expectations. But many of these expectations are superfluous and redundant. So you have to ask yourself whether these norms and beliefs align with your values and priorities. If they don't, be bold enough to say so and agree with your spouse not to implement them. For instance, some cultures expect the friends of the 'husband-to-be' to arrange a stag party for him on the eve of his wedding. Most stag parties are opportunities to get drunk and play silly X-rated games. Well, why would you agree to do something like that if you don't drink and you don't have any plans to mess around with erotic belly dancers? Just say, "No, thank you!"

5. Prioritise What Matters Most.

Before you start planning the wedding, sit down with your partner and talk about what you want the wedding to mean to both of you. Ask yourselves a few essential questions like:

- What type of wedding do we actually want?
- Should it be a small, intimate gathering or a huge, grand affair?
- What kind of atmosphere would we enjoy?
- How do we want our guests to feel?
- What things are non-negotiables and what can we compromise on?
- How much can we realistically afford to spend without getting into unnecessary debt?

Decide what you consider to be the most important aspects of your wedding. Is it the venue, the food, the vows, the video recording of the event, or the photographs? This conversation is crucial because it lays the foundation for everything else. Once you are clear on your shared vision, it's much easier to decide where to spend your time, energy, and money.

In the end, planning your wedding isn't about perfection, but about focusing on what's meaningful to you as a couple. By prioritising your **vision** for this special day, the guest experience, your personal happiness, and the amount you have to spend, you will ensure that your wedding day is truly memorable for yourselves and everyone involved.

6. Plan for the Unexpected.

As you know, nothing in life is certain. So, having a backup plan for those eventualities is prudent. Whether it's bad weather, or car problems, or a vendor cancelling at the last minute—having a contingency plan in place for key aspects of your day can save you a lot of stress. Take a few minutes to think of things that can go wrong and mentally think of alternative solutions, so you're not caught off guard. This is not to make you anxious but to reinforce the idea that your wedding day will go on just fine—no matter what happens.

7. Remember What the Day is Really About.

Amidst all the planning, it's easy to forget that your wedding day is about celebrating your love and commitment to each other. It is also about receiving the grace and wisdom of God to 'do' marriage well. Keep this in mind, and it will help you stay calm and focused on what truly matters. I call it the Big Picture of marriage.

Remember that the wedding is just one day, and that day has very little bearing on the marriage itself. In other words, the wedding day is minuscule compared to the life commitment of marriage. If you and your spouse keep this in mind, your energies will be spent more profitably developing the character and patience you both need to make the marriage a resounding success.

8. Take Breaks from Wedding Planning.

Don't allow yourself to get too consumed by the planning process. Instead, schedule regular date nights or time away from wedding discussions to relax and enjoy each other's company. For instance, you can agree to make Sundays or Fridays a wedding discussion-free day. This will help you keep the wedding planning from taking over your lives.

9. Limit Opinions from Others.

Everyone will have an opinion about your wedding, but too many voices and opinions can be overwhelming. While it's fine to seek advice, make your decisions based on what you and your partner want, rather than trying to please everyone. The truth is that you can't please everyone anyway. So do what you love and appreciate! And let the chips fall where they may. Limit the number of people you consult, and even then remember that the final decision is always yours. At the end of the day, it's your wedding, not theirs.

10. Communicate Openly with Each Other.

It is so sad to see couples start their marriage on the back of hurt or disagreements. Don't let that happen to you. Always speak to your spouse before you make any big decision—especially one that costs a large sum of money or that was not budgeted for. If you don't, your spouse may feel disrespected or deceived—and their trust in you may be shaken. So, endeavour to maintain open lines of communication with each other and with anyone involved in the planning. Regular check-ins can help avoid misunderstandings and ensure everyone is on the same page.

11. Stay Organised.

Endeavour to keep all your wedding-related documents, contracts, and notes in one place. You can use a physical shoe box or binder, or a digital folder. Use tools like wedding planning apps, checklists or spreadsheets, to keep track of your tasks, appointments, and expenses. Staying organised will make it easier to find information when needed. It reduces the risk of forgetting important details and helps you feel less anxious and more in control. Sometimes, a vendor will tell you one thing and deny it when it's time to deliver on it. If you have written and signed agreements on everything discussed, nobody can pull the wool over your face. So, make the effort to get and stay organised.

12. Stay Positive.

Exercise your faith. Trust God to make all things work together for your good. For instance, I know a couple who decided to book an event space they liked. But it was going to cost them more than half of their total wedding budget. When they went in to pay the deposit, the venue owners explained that they could no longer use it on the day they wanted it because someone else had booked the same date. The couple were very upset, but on their way back home they spotted another venue that was as lovely as the one they wanted; but was half the price. It was closer to their homes and the Church; and had a better deal on the food and accommodation of guests. That's what God can do, when you trust Him, instead of worrying.

"Don't worry about anything; instead, pray about everything." (Philippians 4:6.)

Conclusion:

If you focus on these strategies, you can navigate your wedding planning process with less stress and more joy. Remember, it's not about creating the perfect wedding day—but celebrating your love and commitment and enjoying the process and the journey together.

COUPLES DISCUSSION POINTS

- What new ideas have you learnt from this chapter?

  _____

  _____

- Whether you have started planning for your wedding or not, agree today on which suggestions you would like to implement when the time comes to do so.

  _____

  _____

Your Premarital Journal

What thoughts, ideas, decisions and prayer points would you like to keep a record of after reading this chapter? Write them in the space below:

CHAPTER 9

GOD'S WILL FOR YOUR MARRIAGE

For I know the thoughts that I think toward you, says the LORD, thoughts of peace and not of evil, to give you a future and a hope. (Jeremiah 29:11.)

I would like to conclude with the most important aspect of your marriage life. And that is, knowing what God's will is for your marriage. Many couples go into marriage with a 'hope and a prayer'. They hope things will work out for them and they pray. But that's not enough to make it through all the potential obstacles, setbacks, and disappointments of married life.

You have to know without a shadow of a doubt, what the will of God is —so that you can exercise your faith for it in the days and years to come. The Bible teaches us that faith comes by hearing the Word of God continually. So, as you read each point below, take time to meditate long and hard on the Scriptures I share, Why? Because they are the anchors of your faith.

There will be times when you will need to battle the spiritual forces of darkness that will try to destroy your marriage. At such times, if you don't have God's promises to stand on, you will feel powerless, anxious or overwhelmed. If, on the other hand, you and your spouse take the time to study and discuss the lessons in this section carefully and prayerfully, you will be prepared to tackle any attack of the enemy.

God instituted the marriage union because He plans to bring couples together to worship Him and produce the next generation of worshippers. That's why the first thing God said to mankind in the Garden of Eden is:

"Be fruitful and multiply; fill the earth and subdue it; and have dominion over... every living thing that moves on the earth." (Genesis 1:28.)

Sadly, we also know that sometime later, the Serpent attacked that marriage and tried to isolate the couple from their God, from their wealthy place, and from each other. Well, Satan's agenda has not changed. He is still looking for loopholes in every marriage to exploit. So, here are **ten** things God wants you to know about His **will** for your marriage. Look out for them in the months and years to come.

#1.) **Marriage is God's idea.**

And the LORD God said, "It is not good that man should be alone; I will make him a helper comparable to him." (Genesis 2:18.)

Marriage is not a societal or cultural construct. It is a God-idea. This means that marriage is a beautiful and perfect institution since everything God created was very good.

Genesis 1:27, says: **"So God created mankind in his own image, in the image of God he created them; male and female he created them."**

A few verses later it says: **"God saw all that he had made, and it was very good."** This is why we are called to honour and cherish marriage because it carries God's **mark** of approval and blessings. In Hebrews 13:4, Paul writes:

"Let marriage be held in honour among all, and let the marriage bed be undefiled, for God will judge the sexually immoral and adulterous."

In other words, if you don't honour marriage, you will displease God and give Satan a free pass to mess up your dreams of having a great marriage. But if you see your marriage the way God sees it, you'll be motivated to work at it and cherish it for the rest of your life.

#2.) **Your Marriage is designed to reflect the Relationship between Christ and His Church.**

When people come to your home, they should see a reflection of what is taking place between Christ and His Church. They should observe selfless love and deep honour between the two of you. They should see a husband who is willing to die for his wife and a wife who honours her husband like the Church honours Christ—when the Church has a deep revelation of who Christ really is.

That means God wants your marriage to be built on all the virtues and values that accrue to your account as a result of your relationship with Him. For instance, we should see love, mercy, kindness, forgiveness, patience, sacrifice, respect, tenderness, unity, trust, and so much more in your home. That is God's standard. Don't accept anything less.

When you fight to build your marriage on these values, you can't go wrong. Why? Because you'll be building on the Rock. And that Rock is Jesus Christ Himself. When you build on Him and on His Word, He takes responsibility for your life, sustains your relationship, and blesses you with a marriage that glorifies God.

> **"For wives, this means submit to your husbands as to the Lord. For a husband is the head of his wife as Christ is the head of the church. He is the Savior of his body, the church. As the church submits to Christ, so you wives should submit to your husbands in everything. For husbands, this means love your wives, just as Christ loved the church. He gave up his life for her to make her holy and clean, washed by the cleansing of God's word. This is a great mystery, but it is an illustration of the way Christ and the church are one."** (Ephesians 5:22-26, 32.) NLT.

#3.) Your Marriage is a Covenant Relationship.

"...The LORD was witness between you and the wife of your youth, to whom you have been faithless, though she is your companion and your wife by covenant." (Malachi 2:14.) ESV.

It's important to understand that marriage is a Covenant relationship designed by God. It's not just a human agreement or a casual arrangement. It's a sacred, binding relationship established by God, involving commitments and obligations between the two of you and God Himself. When you get married, you become a blood-bound part of your spouse (and vice versa). The vows you say before God and family should be the glue that binds you together as one eternal entity. That's why God pronounced these powerful words immediately after joining Adam and Eve:

> **"Therefore a man shall leave his father and mother and be joined to his wife, and they shall become one flesh."** (Genesis 2:24.)

As much as you love your parents, the goal of marriage is to leave them physically and emotionally. Why? So you can be fully joined to your spouse physically, emotionally and spiritually. Yes, it's good to care for your parents, but they now come after your spouse. That's God's way, and it is the only way that works in the Kingdom of God.

#4.) Praying together is the spiritual master key to a strong sustainable Marriage.

> **"Do not be anxious about anything, but in every situation, by prayer and petition, with thanksgiving, present your requests to God."** (Philippians 4:6.)

Couples who pray together strengthen their spiritual bond. Statistically, up to 95% of these couples will stay married for life. They don't necessarily have fewer problems or conflicts, but their praying together exposes them to the **whispers** of the Holy Spirit. Because they pray together (say, two, three or four times a week), they are more open to repenting and reconciling with each other. God can reveal His perspectives to them more readily as they ask for His wisdom and guidance.

Couples who don't pray together have forgotten that they have an unseen enemy. One who can't be fought with therapy, strategy, self-mastery or willpower. The only effective way to disarm him is to employ superior spiritual power. And that's what prayer is. That's why James the brother of Jesus, said:

> **"...The earnest prayer of a righteous person has great power and produces wonderful results."** (James 5:16.) NLT.

Prayer invites God into your marriage and helps you listen to His immutable wisdom. You start to mature spiritually, emotionally, socially, and intellectually. You learn to silence your ego, your pride, and your sense of entitlement. When you pray and study the Bible together as a couple, you expose yourself to the transforming power of the Word of God. You honour the God who brought you both together, and He helps you have victory over the challenges you face.

So, make it a priority to create time to pray every day. If you can do it with your spouse every day—that's better! But even if you can't synchronise your prayer every day, make sure you come together at least three times a week to pray. It will help you bond. It will help you get on the same page. And it will keep your marriage very healthy.

#5.) Marriage is designed to unite you and your spouse in the deepest ways possible.

> "The two shall become one flesh; so then they are no longer two, but one flesh." (Mark 10:8.)

Although you are still both individuals, marriage binds you together. This means you can no longer think or behave like a single person. You and your spouse are now one spiritual entity. Your identity and destiny are interwoven. And God wants you to spend the rest of your lives together (in one accord), fulfilling your divine assignments and glorifying God in the process.

Divorce terminates this most sacred process. It's no wonder that God says that He **hates** divorce. I encourage you to hate it too. Keep it out of your mind and your vocabulary. Don't entertain it either. Why? Because divorce is almost as painful as death.

Jesus expressed this truth when He said this to the Pharisees:

> "Haven't you read, that at the beginning the Creator 'made them male and female,' and said, 'For this reason, a man will leave his father and mother and be united to his wife, and the two will become one flesh'? So they are no longer two, but one flesh. Therefore what God has joined together, let no one separate." (Matthew 19:4-6.)

Divorce is a separator. It tears the bond of the Spirit apart. It's the antithesis of God's will for marriage. That's why God hates it. But it doesn't have to be your story. Before you make any significant decisions or take any consequential actions, ask yourself whether it would unite or divide you. If it will cause division, reject it. Endeavour to only choose to do things that unify and unite you in the deepest way possible —because in the final analysis, that is the purpose of your marriage vows.

#6.) Marriage only works when you reject your tendency to be selfish and learn to serve each other sacrificially.

"Anyone who wants to be first must be the very last, and the servant of all." (Mark 9:35.) NIV.

Our sinful nature makes every one of us selfish. The only way to effectively deal with this deep human flaw is to renew your mind to the new nature you were given when Jesus saved your soul. Sadly, many people bring their self-centred nature into marriage. They think that marriage is about the other person making them happy. That kind of mindset never works in marriage. So, instead of looking to be served, decide to go into your marriage with a passion to serve your spouse. When Jesus talked about this Christlike attitude He said:

> **"...Whoever wants to become great among you must be your servant, and whoever wants to be first must be your slave—just as the Son of Man did not come to be served, but to serve, and to give his life as a ransom for many."**

There is no better place than marriage to test this principle out. Because when you intentionally go out of your way to serve your spouse, you create an atmosphere for a reciprocal culture to thrive. In other words, your spouse will tend to **respond** reciprocally to your actions. This reaction is called the **Psychology of Reciprocity**—and it happens naturally in most relationships when we feel indebted to another person for doing something unexpected for us.

Giving back makes us feel good. Feel-good hormones are released into our system, and we activate the Law of Reciprocity. That's why serving your spouse is the only **ethical** way to help your spouse serve you. Your spouse will feel loved and cared for; and nine out of ten times, will work harder to serve you too.

> **"For you have been called to live in freedom, my brothers and sisters. But don't use your freedom to satisfy your sinful nature. Instead, use your freedom to serve one another in love."** (Galatians 5:13.) NLT.

#7.) Your Marriage isn't a Feeling, it's a Commitment and a Sacrifice.

> **"Husbands, love your wives, just as Christ loved the church and gave himself up for her."** (Ephesians 5:25.)

It's a mistake to judge your marriage or your love for each other by how you feel. Why? Because feelings are unreliable, temporary, and temperamental. In the course of your marriage, you will experience a whole spectrum of feelings—from feeling despair to feeling ecstatic. Make sure that none of those feelings affects your commitment or your vows.

Your feelings will sometimes lie to you about the state of your marriage. Don't believe the lies. Your commitment (that is, whatever you say to each other in your marriage **vows**), should always be your true North. That's why it's very important to ruminate on your vows long before you say them. My point is that your commitment (or marriage vows), is the foundation of your marriage, not how you feel. Feelings may fluctuate with time, but the foundation mustn't.

Commitment is a function of your **integrity**. You do what you said you would do because you are a person of your word. Not doing what you promised God (and your spouse), nullifies your reputation as a child of God. That's why commitments require sacrifice.

Marriage isn't about taking; it's about giving. The real joy of giving only happens when you have a servant's heart and have learnt to look out for endearing ways to serve each other in love.

> "**Love is patient, love is kind… It always protects, always trusts, always hopes, always perseveres.**" (1 Corinthians 13:4-7.)

The only way to always persevere is to be willing to make sacrifices. But sacrifices don't happen where commitment is lacking. This is what true marital love is—and does when it is present in your relationship.

#8.) Marriage is where you learn to forgive each other—every day.

> "**And whenever you stand praying, if you have anything against anyone, forgive him, that your Father in heaven may also forgive you your trespasses. But if you do not forgive, neither will your Father in heaven forgive your trespasses.**" (Mark 11:25-26.)

Forgiveness is going to be a key aspect of your marriage. The reason is that there is no way to avoid clashes between two very different people with different upbringings and different likes and dislikes. You will both have misunderstandings and you will step on each other's toes. That's a given! But you can overcome the worst offences and conflicts in your marriage if you learn to forgive quickly—just as God in Christ forgave you. Colossians 3:13, says:

> "**Bear with one another and, if one has a complaint against another, forgive each other; as the Lord has forgiven you, so you also must forgive.**"

If you don't learn to forgive, anger, bitterness and resentment will burn a hole in your marriage. Holding grudges or unforgiveness is like swallowing poison, but expecting your spouse to experience the pain. That's not how it works. Unforgiveness will incapacitate and immobilise you. It will make you ill, and Satan will torment you with it. So, keep very short accounts, and make sure you forgive your spouse 'seven times seventy times a day'.

#9.) Conflict is inevitable, but behaving badly isn't.

> "In your anger do not sin: Do not let the sun go down while you are still angry." (Ephesians 4:26.)

Every marriage endures a level of conflict. It's the stuff marriage is made of, and it's inevitable. If you are a typical couple, you will agree on 80% of issues, and disagree on 20%. I call it the 80:20 principle. You will have different ways of looking at life, different ways of interpreting events, and different ways of viewing money, food, health, education, parenting, spending, and even sex. These are some of the things that may produce conflict in your marriage.

It's important to resolve issues like this quickly and calmly, knowing that your ideas are not necessarily right or wrong, but simply different. If you have opposing views in some areas, you can always agree to disagree without making it a 'make-or-break' issue. Don't allow anger to fester and keeping short accounts helps maintain peace and unity in the home.

Every time you allow your conflict to get nasty or abusive, you are sinning against God and each other. So, learn to see conflict for what it is. It is not an excuse to get angry, enraged or infuriated. It is an opportunity to listen to each other, agree to disagree sometimes or put the issue on the proverbial shelf—until you are both willing to see things from God's perspective.

If each time you have a conflict with your spouse, you shout, abuse, hit, slam doors or demean him or her, you are sinning against God and your partner. If you've ever behaved in this manner, it is wrong. Repent, ask for your spouse's forgiveness, and work hard never to repeat it.

> "Repent therefore and be converted, that your sins may be blotted out, so that times of refreshing may come from the presence of the Lord." (Acts 3:19.)

#10.) God wants You to both be Sexually Intimate.

"The husband should fulfil his wife's sexual needs, and the wife should fulfil her husband's needs." (1 Corinthians 7:3.) NLT.

Physical and sexual intimacy in marriage is a beautiful expression of the love that binds you two together. It's essential for emotional connection, and you should make it your goal to fulfil each other's needs in this area with care and respect. Sex is not just something you do to make babies. In a loving and caring relationship, sex has another function.

Sex is designed for procreation and lubrication. It's designed to lubricate your relationship—especially when things have been strained for a while. But there are many other benefits of good, healthy sex in a marriage setting. Here are a few of them:

Good, healthy sex:

- Strengthens your heart and improves your cardiovascular health.
- Releases feel-good hormones (like dopamine, endorphins, prolactin, and oxytocin) into your system.
- Boosts self-esteem, confidence, self-worth, and feelings of love.
- Increases physical affection and overall relationship happiness.
- Helps you maintain a stronger immune system.
- Enhances communication and emotional connection.
- Reduces stress, anxiety, and feelings of dissatisfaction.
- Improves sleep quality and relaxation.
- Keeps you looking and feeling younger.

Here is how Paul explained it:

"The husband should fulfil his wife's sexual needs, and the wife should fulfil her husband's needs. The wife gives authority over her body to her husband, and the husband

gives authority over his body to his wife. Do not deprive each other of sexual relations, unless you both agree to refrain from sexual intimacy for a limited time so you can give yourselves more completely to prayer. Afterwards, you should come together again so that Satan won't be able to tempt you because of your lack of self-control."

(1 Corinthians 7:3-5.) NLT.

Remember that the key to these benefits is not just how frequently you make love, but the **quality** of the sex you have. Do you both relish the experience? Are you both fulfilled? Do you both prepare the ground by being kind and caring? Open communication, mutual respect, patience, and a genuine desire to enjoy each other are essential components of a healthy sexual life.

Note: Sex can be a difficult subject to discuss when you are courting, but it's important to start the discussion even if you need someone neutral to mediate for you. So make sure you do it. You will not regret it.

COUPLES DISCUSSION POINTS

- If you've had any bad sexual experiences in the past, this would be a good time to discuss it with your spouse. Why? Because your introduction to sex (especially out of wedlock) can affect sexual intimacy within your marriage. So, talking about it, and praying together can produce healing and victory over Satan in this area.

_____

_____

_____

- Discuss what you would do together or individually to learn what you can about the gift of sex, without dishonouring God and your bodies on this side of marriage.

_____

_____

_____

Your Premarital Journal

What thoughts, ideas, decisions and prayer points would you like to keep a record of after reading this chapter? Write them in the space below:

A BEAUTIFUL ADVENTURE

A great marriage is available to you and your spouse. You just need to see it with your eyes of faith. I'll never forget when God opened my eyes to see that I could have an amazing marriage despite my awful history. On that faithful day, I flipped my Bible to Psalms 128, and read the first four verses.

Here is what it says:

> **"Blessed are all who fear the LORD, who walk in obedience to him. You will eat the fruit of your labour; blessings and prosperity will be yours. Your wife will be like a fruitful vine within your house; your children will be like olive shoots around your table. Yes, this will be the blessing for the man who fears the LORD."**

After I read this passage, I heard the Lord say, *"If you walk in obedience and honour me the way you should, your life will reflect everything I've promised you in this passage and more. You will have a lovely marriage too."*

That was it. I had a promise from God that was unmistakable. All I had to do was see it with my eyes of faith, and it would be mine. I can't tell you how confident this promise made me. Well, I'm sharing it with you because I want the Word of God to do the same thing for you that it did for me.

If you respect God's Word and commit to obeying it, you will eat the good **fruit** of obedience. You will prosper and be blessed. Your spouse would be fruitful, and your children would **reap** the benefits of your obedience. In short, this Scripture guarantees that if you honour God, your marriage will thrive! God is not a man that He should lie to you. He will perform His Word in your life if you believe it.

I've been married for over 39 years as I'm concluding this manual, and I can tell you that God has kept every promise He made to me and more. Take time today to ask God to give you a similar promise. When He does, it would probably come with some conditions. Take the conditions seriously—then watch God transform you and give you the marriage you've always wanted.

Jesus said, "If you can believe, all things are possible to him who believes." (Mark 9:23.)

Jesus said, "The things which are impossible with men are possible with God." (Luke 18:27.)

"I tell you the truth, you can say to this mountain, 'May you be lifted up and thrown into the sea,' and it will happen. But you must really believe it will happen and have no doubt in your heart." (Mark 11:23.) NLT.

EXTRA SCRIPTURES TO PONDER ON

Ephesians 5:25-26... "Husbands, love your wives, just as Christ loved the church and gave himself up for her to make her holy, cleansing her by the washing with water through the word..."

Proverbs 31:10-12... "A wife of noble character who can find? She is worth far more than rubies. Her husband has full confidence in her and lacks nothing of value. She brings him good, not harm, all the days of her life."

1 Peter 3:7... "Husbands, in the same way, be considerate as you live with your wives, and treat them with respect as the weaker partner and as heirs with you of the gracious gift of life, so that nothing will hinder your prayers."

Ephesians 5:22-23... "Wives, submit yourselves to your own husbands as you do to the Lord. For the husband is the head of the wife as Christ is the head of the church..."

Ephesians 5:28-29... So husbands ought to love their own wives as their own bodies; he who loves his wife loves himself. For no one ever hated his own flesh, but nourishes and cherishes it, just as the Lord does the church.

1 Peter 3:1-2... "Wives, in the same way submit yourselves to your own husbands so that, if any of them do not believe the word, they may be won over without words by the behaviour of their wives, when they see the purity and reverence of your lives."

Ephesians 5:33... "Nevertheless, let each one of you in particular so love his own wife as himself, and let the wife see that she respects her husband."

Ephesians 5:21... "...Submit to one another out of reverence for Christ."

Galatians 5:13... "Serve one another humbly in love."

Proverbs 12:4... "An excellent wife is the crown of her husband, But she who causes shame is like rottenness in his bones."

Your Premarital Journal

What thoughts, ideas, decisions and prayer points would you like to keep a record of after reading this chapter? Write them in the space below:

OTHER BOOKS BY THE AUTHOR

- **Surplus Money** – How to get out of debt, build lasting wealth and leave a legacy of Abundance
- **Secrets of a Lasting Marriage** – 7 Vital Building Blocks for a Healthy Marriage
- **How to Build a Rock Solid Marriage** – Choices That Will Give You the Marriage of Your Dreams
- **Ten Keys to Effective Communication in Marriage**
- **Stress No More** – 20 Healthy Ways To Reduce Stress, Anxiety and Worry
- **Equipping Your Children for Life** – Tools your Children should not leave Home without
- **Maximising Your Season of Singleness** – Using Your Season of Singleness to Prepare for Marriage
- **Keeping God At The Centre Of Your Marriage** – Simple Ways To Keep God At The Centre Of Your Relationship
- **How to Rescue Your Marriage from Breaking Up** – Avoiding the Ten Major Relationship Killers
- **Find Your Soul Mate God's Way** – Say Goodbye To Dating
- **21 Crucial Things They Don't Teach Young People About Sex**
- **Understand Your Marriage Vows** - What the Marriage Vows Mean and How to Honour Them
- **Why God Wants You & Your Family in a Life-giving Church** – 12 Reasons to Get Involved in a Great Local Church
- **Why Can't We Talk About It?** – 4 Practical Steps to Help Reduce Misunderstandings During Conversations by Shola Peters
- **How to Find a Life-giving Church** – You Can Thrive in

All books are available at reputable booksellers online.

www.ingramcontent.com/pod-product-compliance
Lightning Source LLC
Chambersburg PA
CBHW070843160426
43192CB00012B/2293